Religi

Religious Cohesion in Times of Conflict

Christian–Muslim Relations in Segregated Towns

Andrew Holden

continuum

Continuum International Publishing Group

The Tower Building	80 Maiden Lane
11 York Road	Suite 704
London SE1 7NX	New York NY 10038

www.continuumbooks.com

British Library Cataloguing-in-Publication Data
A catalogue record for this book is available from the British Library.

ISBN-13: 978-1-84706-535-3 (HB)
ISBN-10: 1-84706-535-X (HB)

ISBN-13: 978-1-84706-536-0 (PB)
ISBN-10: 1-84706-536-8 (PB)

Library of Congress Cataloging-in-Publication Data
Holden, Andrew, 1964–
    Religious cohesion in times of conflict: Christian–Muslim relations
    in segregated towns/Andrew Holden.
        p. cm.
    Includes bibliographical references and index.
    ISBN-13: 978-1-84706-535-3 (HB)
    ISBN-10: 1-84706-535-X (HB)
    ISBN-13: 978-1-84706-536-0 (pbk.)
    ISBN-10: 1-84706-536-8 (pbk.)
    1. Religion and sociology. 2. Community life. 3. Christianity and
        other religions–Islam. 4. Islam–Relations–Christianity. I. Title.

BL60.H574 2009
306.6′612709427642—dc22   2008022235

Typeset by Newgen Imaging Systems Pvt Ltd, Chennai, India
Printed and bound in Great Britain by Athenaeum Press Ltd, Gateshead, Tyne and Wear

To my family and friends
With love and thanks

Contents

Preface

In the summer of 2001, a series of disturbances erupted in the northern towns of Oldham and Burnley and in the nearby city of Bradford. These disturbances prompted questions about how a society that is home to an increasingly large number of faith and ethnic groups, all with different beliefs, values and aspirations, can remain cohesive. But the one political issue that has caused Western governments to engage much more readily with faith communities now than in the past is the rise in international terrorism. In the UK, religion and state have always been regarded as separate entities, and this makes the so-called war on terror all the more difficult for politicians to win. Theology is not something that governments do, yet the threat posed by religious extremists both to national security and to community cohesion raises the question of whether religious faith can continue to be treated as a purely private matter. The dialogue that now exists between government ministers and faith representatives is not so much a display of courtesy, but a political necessity.

Though we are right to be concerned about the impact of terrorist activity on public relations, this book is not about religious extremism. Nor is it about Christian or Islamic theology. Rather, it is an analysis of how faith communities, particularly when they work together, can contribute to community cohesion in areas of the country that are blighted by segregation. In the north of England, this segregation manifests itself spatially as well as culturally – a situation which leads to the formation of what has recently been described as 'parallel lives'. The waters are muddied even further by the fact that it is often difficult to separate religious identity from other social markers (especially ethnic membership) and that religious convictions vary within as well as between social groups.

Preface

This work is the product of a 2-year investigation known as *The Burnley Project*. The investigation was commissioned by the Home Office in 2005 and overseen by a team of academics at the University of Lancaster. In the period immediately after the northern disturbances, the Cantle committee (an Independent Review Team chaired by Professor Ted Cantle of the Institute of Community Cohesion) made over 67 recommendations that would provide an important backdrop for strategic planning in local councils and for the formulation of government policy. The Cantle report made little reference, however, to the contribution of faith communities to the restoration of social order or to the relationship between religious and secular bodies. While this is in no way intended as a criticism of the Cantle enquiry, it does reveal some uncharted territory.

I write as a sociologist with an interest in religious identity and social relations. Though I write from an agnostic perspective, I am a strong advocate of the view that faith groups can help to assuage tensions and contribute something of value to the community cohesion effort. At present, there is a serious shortage of scholarly literature on religious unity within the social scientific academy. The two East Lancashire towns in which my research was conducted (Burnley and Blackburn) provided fertile ground for the study of faith relations and for an analysis of the interplay between faith, culture and ethnicity. It should be emphasised that Christian–Muslim dialogue is the main focus of this book for no reason other than the fact that these were the two main faith communities in East Lancashire at the time of the investigation. Although the book is intended primarily for undergraduate and postgraduate students (particularly students of Community Studies, Religious Studies and the Social Sciences), my hope is that it will also be a useful reference source for teachers and lecturers, academic researchers, community leaders, religious clerics, theologians, local government agents, voluntary sector employees and anyone else with an interest in religious cohesion.

Acknowledgements

I would like to express my sincere gratitude to all those people who have helped make this book possible. I owe an enormous debt to my colleagues Dr Alan Billings and Professor Paul Heelas from the University of Lancaster for overseeing my research and for their endless words of encouragement. Thanks also to my friend Professor Linda Woodhead for her support as Head of Department and to Professor Ian Reader for his involvement in the early stages of my research. I am grateful to Wendy Francis and Gillian Taylor for their administrative support and to Beth Broomby and Gill Whitworth from the University Press Office for keeping me informed of media publicity.

I owe a special thanks to the members of Building Bridges Burnley for allowing me to attend their meetings and evaluate their initiatives. Their commitment to faith unity is quite remarkable. Among other things, I will miss their friendship, their endless cups of tea and their interfaith feasts. I hope this book will help them to reflect on their spiritual mission and that it will encourage them to build many more bridges.

Thanks also to the interviewees and questionnaire respondents for taking part in the investigation and for helping me to understand the complexities of religious cohesion. I am especially grateful to the teachers and head teachers of the Burnley and Blackburn high schools for allowing me to conduct the Year 10 survey in the face of the major educational restructuring that was taking place in the two towns at the time of my research.

It would be remiss of me not to thank the Home Office and the Department of Communities and Local Government for funding the investigation and for allowing me to conduct my fieldwork without interference. I hope they feel they have received value for money.

Acknowledgements

My final acknowledgement is the most special. It is to my family and close friends for their enduring love and forbearance. It is to them that I dedicate this work. The completion of this book brings not only huge relief but an opportunity to spend more time with those who mean so much to me.

Andrew Holden

1. Faith partnerships and community cohesion: setting the scene

In August 2005, the Religious Studies Department of Lancaster University was commissioned by the Home Office to undertake a 2-year investigation into the contribution of faith to community cohesion. The study was to be conducted in Burnley – an East Lancashire mill town situated in the Pennine hills of North West England with a population of around 90,000 people. The borough as a whole spans an area of approximately 42 square miles, most of which is open moor land. Like many other towns in northern England, Burnley's history is rooted in the textile industry – an industry that has been in decline since the early 1970s. At the time of writing, the most common sectors of employment were public administration, health and education which collectively provided work for around 28 per cent of the town's population – a similar percentage to manufacturing employment (Census, 2001).

Burnley captured the interest of the Home Office for two principal reasons, both of which are connected. The first of these concerned the high levels of segregation that had characterized the borough for several decades and for which economic deprivation was allegedly responsible; and the second was the inevitable damage to public relations caused by the notorious disturbances (an euphemism in the eyes of most local residents for *riots*) that had erupted in the east of Burnley in the summer of 2001. All things considered, the image of the town was far from positive. The borough council's own publications made reference to a fragile infrastructure, low wage labour and poor educational achievement (Burnley Borough Council, 2001, 2003, 2005b), all of which were believed to have had a damaging effect on public morale and on future economic prospects. What, then, could faith communities do to help improve public relations and how might this contribute to other areas of renewal?

My involvement in the investigation (known officially as *The Burnley Project*) began with a meeting at the home of the Bishop of Burnley some 8 or 9 weeks after my appointment and before the official starting date of my employment. For the previous 18 years, I had worked as a teacher in the post-16 sector; first in a college of Further Education some 10 or so miles from Burnley, then in a large Sixth Form in another neighbouring town. My familiarity with East Lancashire was, I was told, one of the reasons I had been appointed over five other candidates. The purpose of the meeting was to introduce me to some members of *Building Bridges Burnley* (referred to hereafter as BBB) – a local Christian–Muslim partnership that had been established in partial response to the disturbances 4 years earlier (Appendix 1). The BBB committee had requested the support of an academic researcher – someone who would be able to evaluate the initiatives in which the group was involved and who would help with future developments.

Unlike conventional sociological research which is generally confined to the description, analysis and explanation of social issues, this investigation bore all the hallmarks of *action research*. Action researchers adopt a more interventionist role than pure empiricists whose main endeavour is to remain detached from participants in order to avoid influencing the data. Since action researchers are both academics *and* initiators of change, they are inextricably involved in the planning and implementation of policy initiatives. Investigations of this kind are unique in that they allow the researcher to participate in the activities that s/he is evaluating and to use his/her knowledge and expertise to help groups or communities to achieve their objectives. For me, this presented a different kind of sociology to the one in which I had previously been engaged.

The action-oriented nature of the investigation manifested itself in a number of ways. First, the activities in which BBB was involved were, by their very nature, practical. The work of the partnership was of interest to a number of stakeholders including the Home Office, the Department of Communities and Local Government, the local and national media, Lancashire Education Authority and Burnley Borough Council, all of which were interested to know whether interfaith initiatives could improve social relations in the Burnley borough. If the research could demonstrate that faith-oriented initiatives could contribute something of *social* value, there was a good chance that it would help steer the work of BBB in a positive direction. Since each initiative had a short-term goal (albeit with a longer-term vision), I was able to make an active contribution to the planning, implementation and evaluation of interfaith programmes. Second, it was clear that, like all other partnerships, the sustainability of BBB was dependent on financial support. Most of the initiatives in which the team was involved required the completion of grant application forms or, in the case of longer-term projects, the submission of lengthy proposals. My familiarity with government funding criteria proved to be of benefit to those members of the team who had had little previous experience of public sector bureaucracy and who were overawed by administrative procedures. Third, the BBB initiatives had an educational dimension that drew on my professional skills and experience. My former teaching responsibilities had included curriculum planning, peer leadership, target setting, workshop co-ordination and a large amount of tutorial work with young people. I also hoped that my educational contacts in the area would create opportunities for the partnership to extend its school outreach provision and to form new working relationships with other educational providers. This was an investigation that had the potential to shape the community cohesion policy of the borough council and improve social relations across the whole of East Lancashire. I was ready for the challenge.

Methods of data collection

A wide range of primary and secondary research methods were employed throughout the investigation. During the first 2 or 3 months, a welter of information was gleaned from documents that were essential for the purpose of contextualization. Some of these materials were published by the Inter Faith Network for the United Kingdom – an affiliated department of the Home Office whose mission is to promote mutual respect and understanding between faith communities in British towns and cities. I also consulted a large amount of literature on community cohesion since this was a central theme of the investigation and one with which faith partnerships were becoming increasingly associated.

In Burnley, Oldham and Bradford, the bulk of this material was published by borough councils at the time of the disturbances. But community cohesion documents were not the only local authority sources to be consulted. In the period immediately after the disturbances, Burnley Borough Council produced several policy documents addressing neighbourhood renewal and urban regeneration. These publications contained details of all 15 wards including the different levels of social deprivation/affluence, demographic profiles and a huge collection of statistics on housing, employment, crime, health and educational attainment. In addition to these materials, a wide range of documents produced by the voluntary sector provided important background information, some of which were used for purposes of comparison.

Alongside the secondary data, a large amount of primary data was collected to test out the assertions of local newspapers and other mass media. These data were culled from semi-structured interviews, a questionnaire survey of three high schools and field-work notes from meetings and observations.

THE SEMI-STRUCTURED INTERVIEWS

Interviews were conducted with a large number of individuals including BBB committee members, religious leaders, school and college teachers, educational outreach workers and a snowball sample of 40 young residents from the Burnley borough.[1] The interviews with BBB representatives yielded important information about the origin and evolution of the partnership and the initiatives in which its members had been involved. It transpired that while the BBB committee had been keen to promote positive faith relations and had already held some successful events (most notably, an interfaith feast and a Tsunami appeal), much of the officers' time had been spent in the execution of mundane administrative tasks such as preparing accounts and completing funding proposals. The interviews enabled me to assess the viability of other initiatives and to help steer the partnership in a direction that was conducive to its own mission.

The next series of interviews were carried out in Burnley's eight high schools and two colleges and, for comparative purposes, a smaller number of schools and colleges in Blackburn. The interviews were conducted with Heads of Citizenship and/or Religious

Education, two head teachers and four college chaplains. The purpose of the interviews was to establish the nature of faith provision and to assess the extent to which the school/college curriculum reflected the religious diversity of the towns. It transpired from these interviews that while some innovative work was taking place, attempts to promote religious cohesion was patchy and unsustained, even in multi-faith establishments.

The 40 interviews with young people were carried out within the first 12 months of the investigation and provided crucial attitudinal data. The interviewees (20 males and 20 females) were selected from a mix of religious organizations and secular agencies. All 40 participants were aged between 18 and 30 years and all were involved in community initiatives. While some of the interviewees had strong religious convictions, others had none. The sample was selected for the specific purpose of exploring attitudes towards different religious perspectives and to establish whether, and under what circumstances, young people were willing to partake in initiatives that contained a faith element. This would help to ascertain the potential for interfaith dialogue and the form that this might take.

The remaining interviews were carried out with religious leaders, co-ordinators and outreach workers. These interviews yielded important data about the dissemination of religious doctrines and about the leaders' perceptions of their roles. It was clear that leadership styles reflected the very different contexts in which the leaders were working and on their attitudes towards secular modernity. The interviews also helped to elicit the leaders' views on how to encourage young people to take part in religious activities.

THE SCHOOL SURVEY

A high-school survey was carried out in the summer term of 2006; approximately 10 months into the investigation. By this stage, I had collected a large amount of interview data and discussed a number of substantive issues with my colleagues at the university. The interviews with teachers and with young people had revealed some significant differences in attitude towards faith and its potential to contribute to community cohesion. It was clear that Burnley and Blackburn were segregated towns and that this segregation manifested itself most clearly in housing and education. The polarization that had occurred in the boroughs since the late-1960s had led to a situation in which large numbers of people rarely transcended their own cultural, ethnic and religious boundaries. There is still much speculation about whether in a modern age of global migration, advanced media communication and cultural fluidity, younger people from different ethnic and religious groups are starting to understand each other better. Most of the British Asian participants with whom I came into contact were born and educated in the UK, spoke fluent English and held the same aspirations as many of their White British counterparts. My sociological interest in these issues provided the impetus for my questionnaire survey which would help to ascertain the attitudes of high school pupils towards each other's cultural, religious and ethnic traditions and to establish the amount of time that young people spent together on both a voluntary and a compulsory basis. The findings of the survey would, I hoped, provide clues for the formulation of appropriate cohesion strategies and for education policy.

Three schools were selected to take part in the survey, one of which was in Burnley and the other two in Blackburn. All three schools were co-educational, community establishments for pupils between the ages of 11 and 16 years and all were located in urban settings. In order to compare attitudes within and between communities, it was important that the pupils in each school were from different religious and ethnic backgrounds and that the socio-economic profiles were as wide-ranging as possible. After several weeks of piloting, the final questionnaire was distributed to 435 students in their penultimate year of high school. Details of the composition of the three schools along with an analysis of the results are presented in Chapter 2.

FIELDWORK OBSERVATIONS

Throughout the 2-year investigation period, I attended a large number of meetings and events in the two comparative towns. Copious notes were made at meetings held by BBB, the Blackburn with Darwen Interfaith Council (BDIC) and *Churches Together*.[2] These meetings enabled me to keep abreast of local interfaith initiatives and to reflect on which of these seemed to be producing the most success. The notes taken at these meetings were filed in accordance with my main research interests; namely, educational activities, leadership issues and the significance of religious beliefs in the wider community.

My attendance at community cohesion events served a rather different purpose. While some of these events were hosted by the faith partnerships of both towns, others were regional and government directed. Local events included lectures and debates, interfaith feasts, residential workshops and project exhibitions. There were also a number of secular events such as youth days, civic renewal lectures, community cohesion conventions and peace initiatives, all of which welcomed the contribution of faith partnerships. The regional events (some of which were by invitation only) were held in various cities throughout the UK. These included conferences and seminars hosted by government Departments, statutory support agencies, local authorities and voluntary groups. The purpose of these events was to provide a forum for the promotion of community cohesion and to enable the representatives of the various organizations to establish a social network. From a research perspective, the opportunity to listen to religious leaders, project managers and government officials talking about different cohesion initiatives aided the process of evaluation and allowed me to reflect on the contribution that faith partnerships could make to secular society.

The pluralistic methodological approach described in this section provided a complete picture of the opportunities for and challenges to religious cohesion in East Lancashire. As the data began to unfold, two key problems became apparent – problems that would come to dominate the whole investigation. First, there was the issue of how Christians and Muslims could work together to achieve a better understanding of each other's religious perspectives. This was as much an *intra*-faith as an interfaith challenge, and one that remains, for the most part, unresolved. In Burnley, this problem was exacerbated by the fact that religious convictions took a variety of forms and expressions; hence, the starting point was to find some empirical means of establishing the importance of faith among different groups of people. The questionnaire survey and the in-depth interviews provided the methodological tools for this endeavor. The second problem (a product very much of the first) concerned the matter of how BBB could use its resources, human as well as physical, to attract more interest. As far as this investigation was concerned, once some attempt had been made to establish the nature and extent of religious conviction, the feasibility of different interfaith strategies and their potential to attract wider groups of people could be addressed. Reference to secondary data and to fieldwork notes was essential for this part of the inquiry. By studying the history and demographic composition of the two towns, I was able to make an informed judgement of the likely outcomes of initiatives that had been tried and tested elsewhere and of whether these would be successful in capturing the interest of anything other than a small number of enthusiasts. It seemed, on balance, that the best way forward was to help BBB and the BDIC to develop a small number of initiatives and to evaluate these within the relatively short time-period of the investigation.

The pages that follow contain details of the initiatives I evaluated and an analysis of the epistemological issues to which they give rise. Although the research was carried out in only two East Lancashire towns, the findings, I believe, have wider implications. There is no reason to think that the initiatives that worked well in Burnley and Blackburn at the time of this investigation would not work well elsewhere. In this respect, East Lancashire is important for no reason other than the fact that it was a multicultural area with a number of evolving faith partnerships.[3] The key findings of my research will, I hope, provide a better understanding of the relationship between religious and ethnic membership and indicate some possible ways forward for what is one of the most important social and political agendas of the twenty-first century.

Community cohesion

Community cohesion has become a central part of local authority strategic planning, yet it is an illusive and difficult concept. What makes communities cohesive and how can this 'cohesion' be sustained? Clearly, it is not enough that people live in close geographical proximity. They could, for example, remain a collection of individuals that have little or no social contact. Cohesion requires social interaction made possible through a range of formal and informal social networks.[4] The more advanced the networks, the more frequent and dense the interaction, and the greater the degree of cohesion. In the UK, the traditional pillars of society such as the church, working men's clubs and trade unions, all of which helped to create some semblance of cohesion until the late-1960s, have largely eroded. If we add to this the high frequency of social migration and displacement across Western Europe before and after this period, it is not difficult to identify the basis of *in*cohesion and the challenges this presents to local authorities.

While diversity is nothing new, the quest for cohesion matters like never before. London alone is now home to people from around forty national or ethnic groups speaking over 300 languages and embracing all manner of religious faith. At the same time, ethnic conflict, war and international terrorism have given rise to competing claims of belonging and identity both at home and abroad. How, then, can we value diversity and still allow communities to retain their distinctiveness? How are we best able to express commonalities in such a highly pluralistic society? Who should take responsibility for social unity? And how can faith partnerships contribute to the community cohesion effort? It would, of course, be impossible for this book to provide the answers to all these questions, not least because of its primary focus on Christian–Muslim relations. It does, however, explore some of the community cohesion issues that arise from religious differences and consider the implications of these for future developments.

In the UK, the need for community cohesion was heightened by post-war migration. As more people began to import different cultures from South Asia, the Caribbean, the West Indies and Eastern Europe, Britain became an increasingly diasporic nation. For most of these migrant workers, British residence was an avenue to upward social mobility despite large-scale research confirming discriminatory practices experienced by members of BME (Black and Minority Ethnic) groups in housing, health, employment and education (Modood *et al.*, 1997).

Contrary to popular myth, ethnic group settlement has changed little in the UK over the past four or five decades. While economic migration, the pursuit of asylum and the global mobilization of refugees have led to greater ethnic diversity, most BME communities are concentrated in a relatively small number of regions. In England, for example, the majority of Pakistanis live in Birmingham, Manchester and Bradford, while most Bangladeshis, Arabs, Iranians and Africans reside in and around London. Although the population of these ethnic groups has risen since the 1960s, a disproportionate number of their members continue to live in deprived urban spaces.[5] By retreating into close-knit communities, BME residents have managed to create their own distinctive enclaves where, if nothing else, they are surrounded by people who share the same social, cultural and religious values. Many of Britain's urban wards, particularly in the larger conurbations, are now occupied by minority groups who have established their own shops, commercial businesses and places of worship.

In East Lancashire, the influx of several thousand Indian, Pakistani and Bangladeshi migrants between 1964 and 1967 presented a new challenge to community relations. In addition to their (mainly) Islamic beliefs, these new arrivals brought with them distinctive languages, values, dress codes, cuisine and a whole host of other cultural practices. In the decades that followed, the pronouncements of far right-wing groups such as Combat 18, the National Front and the British National Party did little to allay the unfounded fears of the White majority that public services, jobs and even the country as a whole were being taken over by undeserving foreigners. Since 9/11, racially motivated attacks have risen significantly in the UK,[6] and in the 7 days after the July 7 London bombings, race crime in Lancashire trebled with 51 more incidents recorded than in the previous year (Patel, 2007). The challenges to which these issues give rise; most importantly, of how to create a society in which different religious and ethnic groups can live amicably together and of how to address distorted perceptions, lie at the heart of the community cohesion agenda.

It might be helpful at this point to distinguish between *social* and *community* cohesion. Social cohesion has tended to be used more widely than community cohesion in that it emphasizes economic rather than cultural processes. In terms of social policy, social cohesion addresses issues of multiple disadvantage and exclusion resulting in and perpetuated by social class inequalities. Community cohesion, on the other hand, is concerned with divisions caused by faith and/or ethnicity and the increased isolation that particular communities may experience as a consequence of their distinctive national and cultural identities (Cantle, 2005, pp. 47–56; Mitchell, 2006, pp. 1138–49). Most definitions of community cohesion centre around two issues which contain an implicit paradox – the identification of common interests and maintaining respect for difference. The 2001 disturbances led to an independent review chaired by Ted Cantle, the purpose of which was to establish the causes of the disturbances and to make recommendations that would help prevent the formation of 'parallel lives'. Some local authorities took the view that community planning systems including racial equality schemes, crime and security strategies and neighbourhood renewal policies already addressed these issues and that there was little need for change. Others (including Burnley) began to revise their policies and formulate new strategies.

The Cantle committee was keen to identify the similarities and differences between multicultural localities and to consider the implications of these for government policy. The final report published in December 2001 highlighted the economic and social inequalities that were believed to be contributing to the polarization of ethnic groups. The enquiry was multi-faceted and made 67 recommendations to a large number of bodies including regeneration committees, local education authorities, the police service, housing agencies, community organizations and local employers. Its main conclusions were that segregation could only be resolved through improved communication and access to information, the establishment of inclusive policies for dealing with conflict and grievances, better diversity training, innovative codes of practice and active engagement between young people (Cantle, 2001). The report provided an important backdrop for the development of community cohesion strategies across the whole country.

Essential requisites for cohesion

If community cohesion is to become a reality, the principles for its success need to be identified. The northern disturbances left a legacy of negative public perception and tense race relations. Following the publication of a piece of research commissioned by the Burnley Task Force[7] and the Cantle committee, the officers of Burnley Borough Council became aware of the need to address a range of difficult issues including racist attitudes and behaviour, urban deprivation, social exclusion, distorted perceptions of the allocation of public resources and, most important of all, the lack of engagement between ethnic groups.

Like many other local authority departments, the Community Cohesion Unit at Burnley Borough Council responded to the recommendations of the Cantle Report by creating its own pathfinder programme, the purpose of which was to establish the local networks needed to foster better public relations. The council adopted the guidance of the Local Government Association in December 2002 which defined a cohesive community as one where:

- there is a common vision and sense of belonging for all communities;
- the diversity of people's different backgrounds and circumstances are appreciated and positively valued;
- those from different backgrounds have similar life opportunities; and
- strong and positive relationships are developed between people from different backgrounds in the workplace, in schools and in local neighbourhoods.

(Local Government Association *et al.*, 2002, p. 5)

If this definition is to be effective, local authorities must adopt strategies that attempt to strengthen co-operation between segregated communities. There are, however, several factors that can hinder this process including:

- fear – characterized by exclusion and an unwillingness to take an interest in or enter into dialogue with people from different social and ethnic groups;
- the failure to address the complexities of integration and identity;
- dissonance between policy and reality;
- insufficient educational opportunities for marginalized groups;
- failure to secure ongoing funding;
- time constraints as a result both of limited funding and of the pressures placed on managers to deliver speedy results;
- limited opportunities for communities to participate effectively in local initiatives; and,

- unrealistic expectations caused by the mismatch between policy targets and the nature of the initiative itself.

(Burnley Borough Council, 2001)

Difficult though it may be, local authorities must find ways of addressing these issues if cohesion is to be achieved. In the first instance, it is essential that initiatives are planned at local level and that project managers can be trusted to allocate public resources in accordance with need. Attention also needs to be given to the events and activities in which people are being asked to participate and to whether this participation is likely to make them feel compromised. It is unlikely, for example, that members of a BME community will express a willingness to partake in an initiative that denigrates their culture and/or beliefs.[8]

In recent years, debates about how best to achieve cohesive communities have revolved around the concept of *social capital* (Putnam, 2000; Woolcock, 2001; Morrissey, 2003; Gilchrist, 2004). In essence, this concerns connections and associations between different groups of people. The main forms of social capital are:

- bonding capital – an inward-looking form of social capital which serves to reinforce exclusive identities. This describes groups that share common experiences such as friends, family members, ethnic groups and religious fundamentalists. This is good for reciprocity, although in bolstering people's narrower identities, it can produce antagonism towards outsiders;
- bridging capital – a more outward-looking form of capital that arises from connections between different groups of people such as neighbourhoods, civil rights movements, youth groups and ecumenical religious organizations. This helps generate broader identities and creates stronger links with outside agencies; and,
- linking capital – an ability to mediate between different levels of society such as local government and voluntary groups.

(Putnam 2000, p. 411)

Bridging and linking capital have the greatest potential to reduce civil conflict as do attempts to tackle economic deprivation.[9] In this sense, the concept of social capital embraces issues that relate to integration, thus making an important difference to the quality of people's lives. Attempts to create integrated communities must, therefore, maximize human participation and empowerment. Through community-based activities, people become more aware of the culture they have internalized (including myths and assumptions), local political structures, decisions made by those in power and opportunities to improve cultural and ethnic relations. If expectations are realistic, the potential for social harmony will be enhanced, but if they are not, feelings of resentment will fester, giving rise to further conflict and the marginalization of those who see themselves as victims of injustice.

Professionals such as youth workers, cohesion officers, project managers, religious leaders and outreach workers must work hard to ensure that the community strategies they are attempting to implement reflect the common good. For any social capital initiative to be successful, it is imperative that clear principles are agreed and that opportunities to participate extend beyond a specific neighbourhood or community. Top–down projects are less likely to produce positive outcomes than projects that allow participants to take ownership and to communicate directly with stakeholders. The recent pathfinder programmes attempt to achieve this by including project representatives in the decision-making process. This widens the potential for dialogue by allowing group leaders the opportunity to network and to establish links with neighbouring localities. In areas of deep segregation, there is a very real need to include marginalized groups in initiatives that generate social capital.

Community projects are seldom neutral interventions, not least because their implementation is premised on the notion that the exclusion of certain groups is a reality. Towns where disturbances have erupted also find themselves having to deal with resentment and disaffection – consequences of what many see as the failure of those in positions of leadership to engage with local residents. These shortcomings raise concerns about political will and professional competence and will only be addressed through open dialogue and transparent communication. It should be recognized, however, that discrete communities are themselves heterogeneous. Younger people, for example, often hold views that conflict with those of the elderly, while females may approach an initiative in a different way than males. Class, disability and sexual orientation must also be taken into account in the planning and implementation of cohesion strategies. It is only by recognizing divisions within as well as between communities that social relations are likely to improve. The current preoccupation with targets, deadlines and performance indicators seriously reduce the impact of cohesion initiatives in segregated towns and cities. If a common sense of belonging is to be achieved, effective strategies will be needed to facilitate interaction between different social groups.

The contribution of faith to community cohesion

In the light of recent global events, it is becoming increasingly difficult for western governments to take the view that the issues that go to the heart of community cohesion are more to do with class, gender or ethnicity than with religion. While these other social dividers remain important in the contemporary UK, events such as the northern disturbances and the terrorist bombings in London call for a much greater recognition of the role that religious membership might play in triggering political and social unrest. But the analysis of religiosity is no mean feat. Public officials frequently come into contact with representatives of religious bodies, giving rise to issues that require understanding and sensitivity. The challenges becomes ever greater when we consider that faith communities are at different stages of development and that tensions often run high between ethnic groups that also hold strong religious beliefs.

The dominance of Christianity in Europe for the last 1,500 years makes Britain a recognizably Christian country to the extent that even those with only moderate Christian beliefs seldom need to think about what it means to be British and a member of a non-Christian organization. British Muslims, however, are compelled to deal with this issue on a daily basis. Though it is not impossible for minority communities to manage these co-existing facets of their identity (Jews, for example, have had a long history of living as a minority group in most European societies), this is a relatively new experience for Muslims in the UK. We should not underestimate the part that religious beliefs play in strengthening the identity of Muslim communities and in reinforcing social solidarity. At the same time, we need to be wary of the anxieties within the Christian community as it faces a future that is characterized by numerous, more confident and often more assertive secular and religious alternatives.

In February 2004, the Home Office published a document entitled *Working Together: Co-operation between Government and Faith Communities* stressing the value of partnerships between public authorities and religious groups. This is one of the first documents to acknowledge the contribution that religious organizations can make to economic and social development. The Northwest Regional Development Agency (NRDA) contends that even people with strong religious convictions are often unaware of the impact of faith communities on regional prosperity. The NRDA substantiated this in its own survey of more than 2,300 such communities in 2003 – a survey that attempted to canvass every place of worship in the region (Northwest Development Agency, 2003). The communities that participated were those classified by the Multi-Faith Centre at the University of Derby and the Inter Faith Network for the United Kingdom. These included Buddhism, Christianity, Hinduism, Islam, Jainism, Judaism, Sikhism and Zoroastrianism. For comparative purposes, Christianity was sub-divided in to nine denominations; namely, Roman Catholic, Anglican, Methodist, Baptist, United Reformed, the Society of Friends (Quakers), the Salvation Army, Evangelical (including Charismatic and Pentecostal) and 'Other Christian'.[10] The survey received an overall response rate of 54 per cent. Outside London and the South East, the North West had the largest population of any English region with nearly 7 million inhabitants.

The survey findings have important implications for government policy. The study showed that virtually all faith community activities were undertaken by volunteers and that the biggest contributions were in deprived urban spaces. It was in these spaces that vulnerable groups such as the homeless, the disabled and the elderly received the greatest assistance. Many faith-based projects were instrumental in fund-raising and in their support for social and environmental issues, confirming that they were key agents of care in the community and important contributors of regeneration. Moreover, a high percentage of tourism in Britain was attributed to the attraction of listed buildings (owned mainly by the Church of England), while at local level faith communities were strong patrons of the arts and sport. In February 2005, the NRDA presented a financial summary of the income generated by those faith groups included in the survey. The report estimated that faith communities in the Northwest region generated between £69.6 and £94.9 million per annum (Northwest Development Agency, 2005). This included the amount of time devoted to health, care and community projects. It also included income generated by religious bodies and revenue collected from religious tourism as shown below:

- Between £60.6 and £64.4 million was generated from the efforts of around 45,667 religious volunteers who contributed a total of around 8.1 million hours. Most of the activities involved work with older people, young people, children and toddlers;
- Cathedrals, museums, retreat houses and a large number of listed buildings attracted around 1.5 million visitors a year, particularly in tourist areas, generating a total of £8.4 million;
- Premises made available by faith communities (particularly Christian denominations) for public use generated between £574,755 and £811,472.

(Ibid., pp. 2–4)

These findings vindicate religious groups from the claim that they have little to contribute to public life and that the acceleration of secular forces will inevitably lead to their extinction. While no-one would question the overall decline in religious *participation* (particularly church attendance) over the past few decades, it should not be forgotten that 76.8 per cent of British citizens identified themselves as belonging to a religious group in the 2001 census. The unprecedented levels of volunteering taking place within and between religious organizations suggests that there are large numbers of people involved in religious activities other than worship. Religious groups are, in fact, starting to be recognized for the contribution they make to regeneration programmes and for the skills and services they bring to local strategic planning. In 2003, religious organizations participated at board level in 7 out of 10 local authorities within the Greater Manchester conurbation and with very little financial support.[11] Volunteers from the faith sector are, however, starting to receive recognition for the contribution they make as providers of pastoral care and advocates of social justice and there is a widespread agreement between statutory agencies that the work of these communities has social value.

The critical perspectives that faith groups can bring to bear on plans for social regeneration have long been underestimated. Religious activities (particularly those facilitated by faith partnerships) can be effective in achieving mutual understanding and mobilizing people into action. The greatest challenge in all this is providing an appropriate context in which people are comfortable in entering into activities with members of other faith communities without feeling that they are compromising their own beliefs. At worst, this exercise will present difficult and challenging questions. At best, it will enable people to discuss their differences and to identify common ground. With enough time devoted to planning and delivery, faith cohesion initiatives can produce empathy, mutual respect and long-lasting friendships. Like all other paradigms that influence the way people view the world, religious beliefs have the potential to unite as well as divide communities, but the prospects of success increase when people are willing to tackle thorny issues.

In virtually every multicultural area in the UK, attempts re being made to encourage members of faith communities to partake in joint ventures. These have taken a variety of forms and are at different stages of development. Within mainstream Christianity, for example, inter-denominational initiatives such as Christmas carol services, world days of prayer, women's forums, charity events and faith sharing groups – all of which come under the banner of *ecumenical activities* – are now well established, even if they are not always well supported. The success of ecumenical activities owes much to the evolution of orthodox Christianity over many centuries. Trinitarian churches, because they derive from the same apostolic tradition (expressed in the Nicene Creed), have a reasonable understanding of each other's history and psychology. It should also be remembered that Christianity, however much it may have weakened, remains the dominant religion of the West, and as such, it appears less strange to the indigenous majority than do small sectarian movements or non-Christian organizations.

The opportunities for the establishment of *interfaith* as well as interdenominational partnerships are also growing. In the UK, there are now over 130 interfaith forums and several branches of national bilateral and trilateral organizations.[12] The most common examples include:

- *Faith Leaders Groups* – these involve liaison between representatives of religious communities who speak with a common voice on issues such as peace, justice, anti-racism, care in the community and a range of global issues;
- *Project Groups* – these are set up to bring religious perspectives to bear on youth projects, community schemes and educational initiatives;
- *Partnership Groups* – make an important contribution to local government initiatives including community cohesion, neighbourhood renewal and urban regeneration. In recent years, religious groups have also become increasingly involved in local authority strategic planning;
- *Spiritual Journey Groups* – these are usually informal groups that operate at parish level. Their main purpose is to raise an awareness and understanding of other religious traditions in order to improve faith relations.

It should be emphasized that these are not fixed categories. Faith partnerships vary in size and some groups may be involved in several activities. There are, however, certain factors that may inhibit the development of a partnership or deem it unsuitable for the operation of certain tasks. Project groups, for example, may lack the expertise required for working with young people or with the elderly and this could limit the impact of their mission. Conversely, internal structures may be insufficient for some interfaith networks to achieve representation on local authority committees – an issue that is not so important for groups merely seeking to learn about other religious organizations. Fundamental to all this is the problem of defining a faith community and of which groups to include. Members of pagan and New Age movements, for example, may regard themselves as people with a deep sense of spirituality, but they often find themselves excluded from interfaith networks either because of their informal structures or because of their unconventional beliefs and practices. According to the Northwest Development Agency (op. cit, 2003 pp. 88–89), the main barriers to interfaith participation include:

1. *Practical barriers* – different faith communities and the various denominations within them are differently structured and organized. This presents problems such as how to include atomized groups in order to ensure that the network is representative. Moreover, some groups may be active outside the authority or may cross the spatial boundaries of the area in which the network has been established;
2. *Agency barriers* – which stem from the indifference of statutory and voluntary bodies. While most departments in these sectors are supportive of faith networks, some remain cautious and/or sceptical. Faith communities that are renowned for proselytizing, for example, may antagonize other religious groups and local authority committees. This may compound the view that they have little to contribute to the wider society and that they are a hindrance rather than an asset to community cohesion;
3. *Capacity barriers* – these derive from the suspicions mentioned under (2) above, for which some faith groups may need to accept responsibility. To a greater or lesser extent, tensions continue to exist between faith communities and secular agencies or even between faith communities themselves. In East Lancashire, however, Christian and Muslim leaders are beginning to engage more actively in dialogue whatever contact they have with lay members. If faith partnerships are to achieve their full capacity building potential, they will need to find new ways of engaging both with their own communities (particularly with disaffected members) and with secular bodies.

In the last analysis, faith groups will only form successful partnerships if they are willing to embrace differences, and these vary in accordance with social context. The exploration of common themes and the ways in which these can be attached to secular agendas will determine the extent to which groups such as BBB are able to tackle segregation and contribute to other areas of renewal. But this will also depend on the personalities of the individuals who are looking to lead the way and on the willingness of outside bodies to allow people of faith a voice. Despite the laudable efforts of faith partnerships in Burnley, Blackburn,

Nelson, Oldham and Bradford to contribute to Citizenship Education programmes between 2003 and 2007, the involvement of older people in faith projects was, during the same period, sporadic and short-term because of insufficient funding and the failure of secular thinkers to recognize the value of faith-based initiatives. By drawing on the data collected during the investigation, this book aims to unravel some of the ways in which faith communities can work successfully both with each other and with the wider society.

Models of religious cohesion

Although empirical research on faith partnerships is in its infancy, it is clear that faith groups can, with sufficient physical and human resources, make an effective contribution to community cohesion. To the religious sceptic, the increasing need for faith communities to draw support from each other is itself evidence of secularization (an issue for sociologists of religion rather than public and/or community sector employees), but it is the *modus operandi* of these partnerships rather than their formation that is of interest here. This book offers an analysis of some of the interfaith strategies that were adopted by BBB and the BDIC between 2005 and 2007 and the impact of these on community relations.

Throughout the investigation, I evaluated a number of initiatives, each of which represented different examples of religious cohesion. From these examples, I have formulated three models which I have called the *dialogical,* the *experiential* and the *contributory.* While all three models describe different ways of promoting religious cohesion and/or of raising the profile of religion in secular contexts, it is possible for a single initiative to meet the description of more than one model. In this respect, the models are intended as a framework for the analysis of a wide range of (but by no means all) interfaith strategies rather than a formulaic system of classification. I have used the example of Christian–Muslim partnerships to illustrate the models because these were the two main faith communities to participate in the initiatives I evaluated.

The dialogical model is the most customary approach and involves the formal discussion of religious doctrines. Although interfaith dialogue often takes the form of a public debate, the events themselves invite guest speakers to offer a summary of their beliefs to a small group or audience. In most cases, the speakers, be they religious leaders or lay people, present their beliefs within a fixed period of time (perhaps around 20–30 minutes), after which they are encouraged to engage in conversation with each other and/or with an audience. The dialogue is aided by formal questions or open discussions which help raise awareness of religious beliefs and/or promote religious unity. The most successful dialogical events are those that allow speakers and delegates the opportunity to explore common ground *and* to air religious differences.

The experiential model is the least formal of the three approaches and takes a wider variety of forms than the dialogical model. Experiential activities include interfaith projects, festivals and exhibitions, residential workshops and educational initiatives. The aim of these activities is to facilitate interaction between members of different faith communities and to invite secular thinkers to engage with religious devotees. Paradoxically, interfaith events that extend their invitation to wider communities often make little reference to religious beliefs on the grounds that this may be seen as an opportunity to proselytize. Religious organizations that host feasts in local places of worship may do so as a gesture of hospitality for local residents, but in the hope that this might also help tackle segregation in areas of civil unrest. When working together, on the other hand, faith communities may express an interest in creating a joint project such as an interfaith exhibition, a celebratory event or a fund-raising appeal. In short, the experiential model emphasizes *doing* rather than, or as well as, conversing.

The contributory model is concerned with how faith partnerships can influence social policy and/or the delivery of public services. In this model, I emphasize the relationship between religious organizations and secular bodies and the promotion of faith through secular activities. Most local authorities across the UK now invite faith partnerships to contribute to strategic planning and encourage them to form alliances with public sector organizations in the hope that this will aid community relations. At the time of my research, BBB was already represented on a number of local partnership groups including East Lancashire Together (ELT), Burnley Action Partnership (BAP) and Burnley Community Network (BCN), details of which I will discuss in

Chapter 5. By entering into these new partnerships, faith communities are able to engage more effectively with secular agents and establish closer links with other stakeholders. Between 2001 and 2007, faith partnerships in East Lancashire made a significant contribution to neighbourhood renewal, community development, hospital chaplaincy, the school curriculum and a wide range of pastoral services in the third and voluntary sectors. The current evidence suggests that it will be the ability of faith communities to extend this provision that will be of greatest interest to secular fundholders.

Each chapter of this book explores a different aspect of Christian–Muslim relations. In Chapter 2, I use some of the fieldwork data to highlight the challenges of uniting young people in segregated towns and cities. The chapter considers the interplay between faith, culture and ethnicity and presents a typology of the religious attitudes of young adults. The chapter continues with an analysis of the negative (sometimes racist) views of school pupils unearthed by the questionnaire survey, the results of which received national media publicity. Disturbing though these results were, it was only by carrying out an attitudinal survey of this kind that the potential for faith partnerships to contribute to community cohesion could be established. In Chapter 3, I consider the implications of the negative views described in Chapter 2 for education policy and examine some of the ways in which schools and colleges can tackle these issues. My examination is based on examples of classroom delivery and outreach provision. In Chapter 4, I present a case study of a project for young adults known as *The Spirit of the North* – an interfaith initiative that had already been launched in eighteen towns in the north of England prior to my appointment. This initiative was reaching its completion stage in Blackburn at the beginning of my fieldwork period and arrived in Burnley several weeks later. The interactive nature of the initiative and the different ways in which it was approached by the participants makes for an interesting comparative analysis and provides an insight into how religious projects aimed at young people can attract the interest of wider audiences. Chapter 5 addresses the issue of faith leadership and considers how the changing religious landscape of the UK affects the work of Christian and Muslim clerics. The chapter contains attitudinal data from young adults about the effectiveness of religious leadership and the new directions that this will need to take if faith leaders are to play a more active role in the life of the community. The chapter presents the views of religious leaders themselves and examines some of the interfaith leadership initiatives established in East Lancashire towards the end of the investigation. The concluding chapter considers possible ways forward for Christian–Muslim relations in Britain and for the development of new partnerships between religious and secular bodies.

Before the 2001 disturbances, there was little if any alliance between different religious and ethnic groups in the north of England and the absence of an appropriate forum through which people could air their grievances. One of the biggest challenges facing statutory, voluntary and religious organizations in the UK at the beginning of the twenty-first century is the question of how to provide opportunities for communities to work together in order to improve social relations. This will not be achieved through a national agenda that espouses total integration or by running local affairs in an exclusive manner. Initiatives that aim to promote social justice and create positive attitudes need to be established across the whole of the public sector, and this can only happen in a climate in which people do not feel that they are in competition with each other or threatened by each other's ways of life. Religious groups have an important role to play in this agenda. In areas of the country where there is a high degree of mistrust between communities and where world events have had a negative effect on people's attitudes, Christian–Muslim partnerships can be a conduit through which to tackle segregation.

Notes

1 Pseudonyms have been used throughout the book to protect the identities of the interviewees.
2 *Churches Together* was a consortium of mainstream Christian denominations in both towns.
3 See Appendices 2 and 3 for details of the faith and ethnic group composition of Burnley and for the comparative town of Blackburn.
4 For a detailed discussion of the relationship between social structure and patterns of community, see Tonnies (1887) and Frankenburg (1966).

5 Despite the fact that the UK was able to offer a higher standard of living to these communities in the post-war period than their former homelands, the low-skilled employment in which they often found themselves was a source of poor-wage labour, making desirable housing in the more affluent areas unaffordable. The privately rented sector was thus the dominant mode of tenure for most Black and Asian minorities.

6 Prior to 9/11, there were around 30 incidents of Islamophobia reported in the UK each year compared with around 450 incidents per year afterwards (Patel 2007).

7 A committee set up to investigate the causes of the disturbances and chaired independently by Lord Anthony Clarke.

8 It should also be noted that people may choose to live in segregated communities because they feel more comfortable living alongside those with whom they share a common identity. This makes cohesion all the more difficult to achieve.

9 For an analysis of the difficulty in moving from bonding to bridging capital, see Leonard 2004.

10 The questionnaire was a more detailed version of the one used in a previous survey undertaken by the London Churches Group in 2002.

11 Of the religious organizations that took part in the 2003 survey, only 27 per cent had received public funding.

12 *The Council of Christians and Jews* and *The Three Faiths Forum* are among the best-known national examples.

2. Religious attitudes among young people

If Christian–Muslim unity is to be advanced in times of conflict, there needs to be some attempt to explore the possible forms that this might take and to measure its potential for future development. The attitudes of young people towards religious beliefs and religious leaders are useful indicators of the general status and future trajectory of religious cohesion. There are several ways in which these issues can be investigated – visits to schools and colleges, focus group research, questionnaire surveys and so forth – all of which produce different kinds of data for social scientists and policy makers.

In the early stages of the investigation, some crucial questions began to emerge, all of which lent themselves to research among high-school pupils and young adults. Interviews with school teachers had already revealed that while pupils received knowledge of world religions through the RE curriculum, faith in the form of worship or as an implicit part of the school ethos depended largely on whether the school had a religious or secular constitution. Outside school, there was much evidence of spatial segregation in East Lancashire – a reality that had done little to aid faith and ethnic relations since the mid-1960s. The questions that needed to be addressed concerned the relationship between religious and community cohesion and whether the former could be shown to contribute something positive to the latter. For example: Were the young people of East Lancashire present in any significant numbers in places of worship? What knowledge did they have of religious differences? What views did they hold of religious diversity? At what point did religious cohesion spill into the issues of integration and multiculturalism? What was the extent of the social contact between young people from different religious and ethnic communities? If alienation was widespread, did this have a religious basis or was religion only a secondary marker? What value, if any, did young people with secular views place on religious activities that aimed to bring segregated communities together?[1]

The data for this chapter were collected through two principal means – semi-structured interviews and a questionnaire survey. The interviews (40 in total, each lasting between 1.5 and 2 hours) were carried out during the first 12 months of the investigation and transcribed in the summer of 2006. These were tape-recorded interviews that produced qualitative material from young adults between the ages of 18 and 30 years. Though it would be naïve to suggest that a sample of 40 people is in any way representative, consideration needs to be given to the fact that interviewing is a time-consuming exercise that requires organization and planning. For the purposes of this investigation, the main strength of semi-structured interviews lay in the fact that the same set of open- and closed-ended questions could be asked of respondents and could, therefore, be used as a comparative tool.

The questionnaire survey was administered in three high schools towards the end of the 2006 summer term. Unlike the interviews with young adults, the survey produced data from a much larger group of young people (435 in total) in their penultimate year of secondary education. The majority of the pupils were 15 years of age at the time of the research and all attended community rather than voluntary aided schools. One of the objectives of the survey was to examine the relationship between religious tolerance and ethnic membership; hence, the three schools were selected on the basis of pupil profiles. The data elicited from the interviews and the questionnaires have been presented in the same chapter to give a more rounded picture than if they were presented separately. This combination of quantitative and qualitative material enhanced the validity and reliability of the data, making the findings more generalizable. The adoption of both methodological approaches allowed the overarching questions of the investigation to be systematically and rigorously tested.

Defining the markers of identity

Before embarking on a discussion of the key findings of the investigation, I want to address three forms of social division which tend to be treated (quite wrongly) as if they were the same phenomenon.

These are *religion, culture* and *ethnicity*. If we are to acquire a better understanding of the causes of social segregation and of how faith partnerships might help to engage with secular as well as religious communities, the analysis of these three different aspects of identity needs to be much more nuanced.

As the investigation started to unfold, I became aware of the fact that although Burnley and Blackburn were segregated towns, people seldom made reference to *religious* divisions. One of the views most frequently expressed by the interviewees was that religious beliefs were a largely private matter and that the towns were segregated not so much by religious faith, but by culture and ethnicity. Moreover, there was little mention (not least, I suspect, because there was little awareness) of divisions *within* as well as between communities. Although there were many similarities in the interviewees' descriptions of the two towns, these descriptions tended to be general and simplistic, expressed in the language of 'them and us' and indicative of the bipolar demography of the boroughs.

Despite media coverage of the religious violence associated with Al-Qaeda and other terrorist groups since 9/11, Christian–Muslim relations in the UK remain largely positive. This is due, in no small part, the rejection of radical Islam among most British Muslims who express an earnest willingness to work with other faith groups in the pursuit of community cohesion. At the same time, the declining significance of Christianity at both macro and micro levels has reduced the potential for religious conflict and accentuated other forms of segregation.

While social class cuts across almost all other social dividers, it is ethnic division that has manifested itself most visibly (often in the form of civil disturbances) in areas of high-economic deprivation. For die-hard Marxists, ethnic tensions have their roots in economic inequality and are triggered by growing frustrations among marginalized groups. In East Lancashire, where there is a long history of educational underachievement, high levels of social exclusion, strong British National Party (BNP) influence and competition for scarce resources; the struggle for a better quality of life has fuelled ethnic conflict and deepened the social divide. The bipolar organization of a large number of East Lancashire towns into two distinct ethnic groups deflects attention away from internal divisions and gives the impression that Asian and White communities are single separate entities with their own reified cultures.

Ethnicity is a concept fraught with confusion. Although the term is often used in relation to racial identity, strictly racial (or biological) attributes are not necessarily, or even usually, a feature of ethnic membership. Most definitions of ethnicity refer to shared language, national loyalty or common homeland. In the East Lancashire boroughs of Burnley, Pendle and Blackburn, the largest BME groups are Indian, Pakistani and Bangladeshi, but these are sub-divided by caste, class, culture, religion and language. It makes no sense, therefore, to describe Muslims living in these boroughs as an ethnic group.

Unlike ethnicity which is based mainly on national identity, culture is a collection of shared characteristics and symbols that constitute a way of life. While culture can be attributed to whole societies, it is more commonly associated with communities (or even communities within communities). We do, however, need to be wary of dominant discourses of culture which tend to be stereotypical and misleading. To make general statements about 'Asian', 'Jewish' or 'Irish' culture, for example, is to ignore important distinctions in value systems, loyalties and political allegiances which stem from migratory history and from a complex range of regional and sociological cleavages. In East Lancashire, some of the most recent cultures have been born out of territorial gang rivalry in which age and ethnicity transcend religious membership. These gang cultures (commonly referred to by sociologists as youth or 'street' cultures) have their own distinctive rites of passage, yet they have emerged at neighbourhood level.

While we must be careful not to conflate ethnicity, culture and religion, we need to bear in mind that each of these is of greater or lesser significance in the formation of communities and that there is a pivotal relationship between the three. Groups such as Black Pentecostalists, Irish Catholics and Pakistani Muslims may synthesize their ethnic and religious identities in certain social contexts, yet form 'cultural' alliances with other communities with which they come into contact. It may also be fair to suggest that while religion may be more divisive than culture among adults, this is seldom the case among teenagers. The wide-ranging criteria that people draw upon in their attempt to establish a secure sense of belonging and maintain affective bonds with those with whom they share common characteristics highlights the challenge of achieving cohesion in segregated urban spaces.

The importance of religious beliefs to young adults

The 40 interviewees were selected from different places of worship and from a large number of secular organizations. Since the aim of this part of the investigation was to explore attitudes towards religion and its potential to create a cohesive town, it would have been a mistake to target only those with religious convictions. One of the most interesting questions, it seemed, was whether young people with essentially secular views placed any value at all on faith relations – a recognition that would itself be indicative of religious tolerance and would give due consideration to the fact that non-believers (some of whom regard themselves as 'spiritual' rather than religious) often endorse principles that derive from the Judaeo-Christian and Islamic traditions. It followed that if religious *tolerance* (in this case, a willingness to listen to and to make some attempt to engage with people for whom religious beliefs holds some significance) was high among non-believers, then there was a strong rationale for including religious sceptics in certain faith-oriented activities.

A total of 20 White and 20 Asian interviewees (10 males and 10 females from each group) were selected from local churches and mosques and from various NGOs[2] involved in community projects. This meant that although the interviewees who held religious convictions belonged to different religious and ethnic groups and attended different places of worship, their involvement in secular projects brought them into regular contact with each other. Several of the interviewees were members of the same steering committees and were involved in the same strategic partnerships and it was from within these contexts that those of no faith were invited to take part in the investigation. The final group of interviewees could, therefore, be described as a snowball sample of young adults from the town's two main ethnic groups and from a wide range of religious and non-religious backgrounds. Of these two ethnic groups, it was the Asian interviewees who were most likely to express their identities in religious as well as in ethnic terms, but they too varied in their religious convictions and in their views on faith relations. This suggests that we should be wary of defining people solely by religious membership and that religious cohesion in segregated towns is not necessarily achieved by focusing on faith alone, but on other dividers such as age, gender, ethnicity and locality.

Like all social scientific research, this investigation involved value judgements about who to involve, how they should be selected, what questions should be asked and what issues were worthy of analysis. Attention also needed to be given to the heterogeneous religious landscape and to the fact that religious attitudes took a variety of forms. My decision to select an equal number of individuals from the two main ethnic groups was motivated not only by the need for representativeness, but by the fact that it was youths (or to be more specific, young males) from within these two communities that had been the main protagonists of the 2001 disturbances.[3] The selection of the final group of participants was not, however, a purely random exercise. In the preliminary stages of the investigation, I held a number of discussions with youth workers and community leaders who helped to create the final sample by providing me with the names and contact details of prospective interviewees. I then held some informal conversations with the individuals themselves to establish religious, ethnic and socio-economic profiles and to confirm people's willingness to take part in the investigation.

The 40 participants were interviewed individually and asked a series of questions about their lives as local residents. At the beginning of the interviews, the respondents were asked to share their biographical narratives (that is, details of family relationships, childhood memories, educational experiences and personal and professional development) since leaving school. The interviews then progressed to questions of an existential nature, at which point, the respondents described their religious perspectives and (where applicable) details of their faith journeys. The interviewees were asked about their perceptions of faith partnerships and about what they felt people of faith could contribute to community cohesion. Those with religious convictions were asked to comment on other religious groups and to identify what they thought were the main similarities between Christians and Muslims. The most important questions concerned the amount of contact, voluntary or otherwise, that the interviewees had had with members of other religious and ethnic groups. The data were then used to ascertain attitudes towards community cohesion by a range of descriptors including religious membership, occupation, ethnicity, gender and locality.

To date, religious attitudes have not been well theorized within the social scientific academy. Nor have policy makers or even religious groups themselves made any serious attempt to establish how faith perspectives come to be acquired. I found that young people's perceptions of religion and its potential to create a better society varied in accordance with locality and with levels of integration. In the case of the White majority, it was clear that even those with no religious convictions but with a strong appreciation for cultural diversity (especially those who had frequent contact with people of Asian heritage) were able to recognize the importance of religious beliefs in the lives of others far more easily than those who failed to venture outside their own comfort zones. Among most of the Muslim respondents, there was a complex interplay between religious, cultural and national identity which was poorly understood by secular thinkers and by those who had little contact with minority ethnic groups. This highlights the need not only for religious and ethnic communities to engage more frequently with each other, but for people of no faith to understand that religious cohesion can benefit secular society. The following typology may help to illuminate some of these diverse religious and non-religious perspectives.

A typology of religious attitudes

While typologies are often criticized for their generalized and over-simplistic representations of social phenomena, they do, none the less, provide a starting point for the analysis of social attitudes. The typology below is an attempt to chart different faith perspectives and to demonstrate the extent to which secular as well as religious thinkers are willing to take part in discussions, events and activities that promote religious cohesion. The following 'types' have been identified from the analysis of a wide range of primary source material including interview data, conversations with residents, evaluation questionnaires administered at interfaith events and the Year 10 survey. Teachers, religious leaders and project managers may find the typology helpful when planning religious and/or community initiatives. Policy makers, on the other hand, may prefer to use it as a template for the investigation of social and political attitudes or as a frame of reference for engaging with faith communities.

The participants who expressed religious views either in interviews or through the questionnaire survey could be divided into four distinctive sub-groups. I have called these *the religious inclusivists, the religious exclusivists, the secular integrationists* and *the secular aversionists*. Each group represents people who hold similar views of religion and who are equally supportive (or equally critical) of activities that contain a religious element. Curiously enough, not everyone with religious convictions expresses a willingness to partake in interfaith dialogue or even to encourage activities that promote religious cohesion. Conversely, there are a significant number of religious sceptics who, despite their agnostic or atheistic views, applaud the attempts of faith partnerships to unite segregated communities and to work in as positive a way as possible with secular agencies. Some of these respondents even express an interest in contributing to faith-based initiatives, as long as there is no inclusion of worship and/or no attempt to proselytize. My findings confirmed a wide variation of attitudes among young people and a complex picture of religious diversity within and between social groups. Extracts from the interview data have been included in order to demonstrate some of these differences and to give the interviewees a voice.

RELIGIOUS INCLUSIVISTS

Religious inclusivists are, as the term implies, people of faith who are willing to engage with members of other religious groups. Most religious inclusivists regard themselves as moderate in their religious behaviour, although the nature of their beliefs and the intensity of their convictions vary. As far as this investigation was concerned, this group represented those who held religious beliefs, regardless of whether they attended a place of worship. Religious inclusivists lived in different localities and were affiliated, for the most part, to mainstream religious communities. Among the Christian denominations, inclusivistic attitudes were widespread among Roman Catholics, Anglicans, Methodists, Baptists and non-conformists. The Muslim respondents expressed an even greater homogeneity of religious attitudes and willingness to work with other faith groups despite their adherence to strict religious rules.[4] As one might expect, the Muslim communities of East Lancashire tended to regard conservative Christians as close allies, recognizing similarities not so much in religious doctrines, but in ethical and moral principles. The following comments from four of the interviewees, two Muslim and two Christian, convey the perceptions that these two communities held of each other and of their mutual willingness to engage in dialogue:

> I think that there are moral values that stem from people's faith and when this comes across, it's fantastic. I have seen a charitable spirit from the Christian community when the Tsunami happened . . . they were out in the town centre collecting with their buckets . . . always willing to give and I think that this is shared across the board with people of other faiths and even no faith as well . . . and I think that if people of different faiths come together, they can be a united force, because there's a push towards secularism in our society and a shift away from faith. (female Muslim aged 24 years)

> Our religion does not block out other religions. In this society, the main religion is Christianity and we don't disrespect this in any way. Some of the things that are taught within Christianity, we believe in and can relate to . . . some of the things we relate to and accept, just like Christianity accepts some of the things that Islam has to offer and some things we might agree to . . . so my religion isn't just Islam, it's Christianity, Judaism and Islam. There are things in Christianity and Judaism that are exactly the same as Islam . . . people talk too much about differences rather than similarities. (male Muslim aged 21 years)

> I think that other faiths have a massive amount to offer. I really believe that different faiths can live together and share life together and share different concepts of their faith together and yet still hold strong in their own faiths. Muslims have offered me so much that has helped my own faith and I think it's very healthy to be with people who are different . . . Muslims have lots of things that can contribute to my faith. One thing is their

commitment to prayer . . . I'm astonished constantly that they manage to pray five times a day and I think that Christians have got so much to learn from that. The Christian church and the Muslim community are working closely together in Burnley and I have seen amazing things happen. In lots of ways, I don't think we're segregated at all apart from different worship centres and so on where we have to be divided; but I think it's a race thing that divides people, not religion. (female Christian aged 23 years)

It's nice to chat with Muslims about their faith. There are things that as a Christian I would object to about other faiths, but I also think that Christians could learn a lot from other people. It was fascinating for me to hear about some of the things that Muslims do during Ramadan and I think there are an awful lot of things we could all learn . . . I think that a lot of Christians eschew discipline and most Christians tend to see discipline as a negative thing. Christians seem to want a dedicated, but not a habitual relationship with God; but the Muslim concept of praying five times a day is something that Christians could get a lot out of. The majority of people don't find prayer easy and I think that if there's something to encourage you, that's no bad thing . . . I would say that the Bible is the truth, but that doesn't mean that we should shun other faiths. I think that we should embrace other faiths. As Christians, we should live in a way that is relevant to the world rather than be isolated from it. I think that I would struggle to pray with other faiths and worship with other faiths, but other than that, I think we have a lot to gain from each other both socially, and in some respects, religiously. (male Christian aged 24 years)

Although there is little reference to doctrinal issues in these commentaries, the interviewees clearly respected their religious counterparts and were eager to engage with other religious groups. The fourth respondent realistically acknowledges the difficulties involved in partaking in joint worship, but is none the less supportive of religious unity. The first respondent suggests that charitable acts such as fund-raising provide one of the best opportunities for people of faith to work together and that this can aid religious cohesion without necessarily having to enter into dialogue. Practical initiatives such as these can be an effective way of uniting people who live in some of the most segregated areas of the country.

In addition to the challenges that faith communities face in working together is the equally difficult task of including people of no faith in religious initiatives. My research showed that the religious inclusivists were happy to engage with agnostics, atheists and secular humanists, but recognized the difficulties of achieving this through liturgy. The respondents' solution to this was to show faith by good example, mainly by participating in community (especially charity) events that worked towards the public good. The general feeling was that while initiatives such as these were not driven by a liturgical agenda, they did at least embrace values such as humanitarianism, social justice and self-sacrifice, all of which could earn the respect of non-believers. The following comments from an interview with a Christian youth officer echo this suggestion:

> It's about having the chance to spend time with people who do not have a faith, but it needs to happen in the right setting. I went to an event recently at the Burnley Youth Theatre. It was an event that was about bringing people from different ethnic groups in Burnley together and I think this should happen a lot more. The people who took part spent the day together and they learnt a lot about community and cohesion and exploring those ideas. There were Christians and Muslims who also took part and they talked about their faith and how this helped them to make Burnley better. The whole day went really well and I think this needs to happen much more. (female Christian aged 22 years)

This young woman's occupation clearly lent itself to the underlying principles of community cohesion and her comments endorse the view that religious perspectives can be incorporated into secular activities. There is, however, one other detail in her commentary that is worthy of consideration and that has important implications for the analysis of segregation. The multicultural event to which she referred was aimed mainly at ethnic groups rather than religious activists and this raises the question of whether it was faith, ethnicity or something else that was responsible for the deepening segregation that was occurring in East Lancashire. When asked to explain the causes of division in Burnley, the majority of the interviewees claimed that it was culture and/or ethnicity rather than religion that divided communities.

Social class has always been one of the main forms of segregation in every human society, but the fact that it cuts across other dividers – age, gender, ethnic membership, religion, nationality and so forth – makes it very difficult to analyse as a separate variable. In segregated areas of the country, class divisions exacerbate other tensions that derive from the often negative perceptions that different communities hold of each other. The nature and extent of social segregation and its complexity in Burnley was expressed by several interviewees:

> I think Burnley is segregated in millions of different ways; but I don't just see it as a Burnley problem, I see it as a worldwide problem. People don't look at how they can relate to each other; they look at differences. I think that Burnley has territorial problems, religious problems and also class problems. Some people feel that they are getting less money from the council and the BNP tell people this . . . then there's racism which is another problem. Some people don't go into Asian areas because they think they'll get beaten up because they're White; and Asians won't go into a White community because they think they'll be beaten up by White people. I think that the riots have caused more and more segregation and there are areas that didn't have a problem with racism before, but they do now because of the riots. (Asian male resident aged 22 years)

> I think that regeneration is a good thing but it's also a bad thing because people are shifting to other areas of the town. When they knock the houses down in White areas, White people won't move into an Asian area; they'll move into another White area. At the moment, Asian people are having their houses knocked down in the Daneshouse area and so what's happening is that they're starting to move into the more mixed area not too far away. But the people in that area are now starting to feel uncomfortable and they're moving away; so people are always shifting away because they're just not used to having different ethnic groups living near them. (White male resident aged 19 years)

When our parents moved to this country, they came here to work and with the idea of going back one day; but things have changed now because the second generation see Britain as their home and Pakistan as a visiting place; so we can't live there because we don't know how to live there. You see, our parents withdrew themselves from society when they moved here. They went to work and then came home and didn't really move out of the areas that they'd settled into and I think that caused a lot of problems. Even now, you get older people from our own communities who won't talk to White people. They'll talk to nurses and doctors and people like that because they have to, but they don't find it easy to make conversation; whereas if I see a White person I'll say 'Hiya' and I think this is where it's getting better. (Asian male resident aged 24 years)

I think it was much more difficult for our parents when they migrated to Burnley in the 1960s because they didn't know the language and this cause fear on both sides; and because they couldn't speak the language, they couldn't mix and so neither party really wanted to mix and I think that this would happen anywhere. But it's certainly getting easier now. It's like asylum seekers who come into this country; they see us as another minority group that are already established and they can relate to us and they're picking up on how to get on with people because they can see that we're doing it. But our parents had no example to follow. (Asian female resident aged 26 years)

These four residents seemed acutely aware of the segregation that existed in their town and all commented on its various manifestations. The issues of insularity, White flight, fear of difference and language barriers were well known to local council officers and community leaders. At present, the greatest challenge facing religious groups is how to make their mission meaningful and applicable to those who are indifferent to faith and who feel that their towns are divided not so much by religion but by culture and ethnicity. While it is not the responsibility of faith communities to tackle economic deprivation, religious leaders can certainly provide personal and pastoral support to those who have experienced some of its worst effects. More generally, faith groups can, with sufficient funding, act as capacity building agents in segregated urban spaces where tensions run high and where people regard segregation as a hindrance to cohesion. It is here that the religious inclusivists can offer some positive ways forward.

The perceptions of the above interviewees highlight the need for strategies that address social divisions. The support for religious cohesion expressed by the respondents can help to assuage fear and suspicion and reduce the potential for civil unrest. If the religious inclusivists are to be successful, however, they must address the main causes of these divisions and find new ways of linking their religious objectives to the community cohesion agenda. In the north of England, faith partnerships have attempted to promote religious tolerance through race relations policies and Citizenship Education. The educational outreach work in Burnley, Pendle and Blackburn (details of which will be presented in Chapter 3) provides one of the best examples. Activities such as team building, role play, empathy workshops and cultural awareness programmes in schools and colleges enables facilitators to incorporate their inclusive philosophy into a range of initiatives for young people. In 2001, the Pendle group produced its own Citizenship Education programme for Year 6 and 7 students in the Nelson and Colne area while in 2002, the *Bridge* team (a sub-group of BBB) introduced a range of after school activities for younger children. These cultural and ethnic diversity programmes reflect the attempts of religious inclusivists to approach faith through ethical values rather than as a moral duty. While traditionalists would regard this as an altogether too subtle approach to religious ministry, it is, in the current climate, the most realistic way of engaging with young people whose attitudes towards religion vary enormously and who seldom see religious division as a source of discontent.

RELIGIOUS EXCLUSIVISTS

Unlike religious inclusivists, religious exclusivists are people for whom interfaith dialogue carries theological risks. While belief in the certainty of one's own doctrines can vary even among religious moderates, exclusivists regard interfaith initiatives as indicative of weak conviction and an attempt to undermine truth. The most exclusive organizations are those that espouse fundamentalist teachings and that use these teachings as the basis for renouncing the world. This is not to say that exclusivists live in closed communities (most, in fact, do not) or that they are unwilling to converse with people who hold different views to themselves, but rather, that they are inclined to keep voluntary contact with outsiders, religious as well as secular, to a minimum. From their perspective, this symbolic separation is a manifestation of spiritual cleanliness and of a desire to show the rest of the world that they are a people set apart. Millenarian movements (that is, movements that prophesy the end of the present world order in anticipation of an impending Day of Judgement) fall into this category. Devotees of millenarian groups regard exclusion as a necessary requisite for their own salvation.

Religious exclusivity can be found in all the major world faiths. At their most extreme, exclusive ideologies can act as a catalyst for religious violence (as in the case of Holy Wars or suicide bombings), though most are expressed in less radical forms. While I found no evidence of religious radicalization in my research (certainly not the kind associated with acts of terrorism), it would be wrong to suggest that religious exclusivity did not exist. In every main town in East Lancashire, there was a small but significant number of exclusive organizations such as the Church of Jesus Christ of Latter Day Saints (the Mormons), the Watchtower Bible and Tract Society (the Jehovah's Witnesses) and a small cluster of Pentecostal and house fellowship churches, all of which preached the importance of religious separatism. These movements are renowned for their dualistic *weltanschauung* (that is, the view that the world comprises the warring forces of good and evil) and for their condemnation of other faith communities. The following two quotations from Jehovah's Witness publications demonstrate some of these characteristics:

Satan has used verbal and physical persecution to turn individuals away from true worship. But he has also employed more subtle means – cunning acts and sly devices. He has cleverly kept a large proportion of mankind in darkness by means of false religion; letting them think, if they so desire, that they are serving God. Lacking a genuine love for truth, they may be attracted by mystical and emotional religious services or be impressed by powerful works. (Watchtower Bible and Tract Society 1983, p. 64)

Thus, by what they have taught and what they have done, the religions of Christendom have demonstrated that their claim of believing in the Bible and of being God-fearing and Christian is a lie. They have betrayed God and the Bible. In doing so, they have disgusted millions of people and caused them to turn away from belief in a Supreme Being. (Watchtower Bible and Tract Society 1993, p. 19)

It is rather surprising, given their scathing attack on other religious communities and unequivocal renunciation of the world that exclusive groups such as the Mormons and the Jehovah's Witnesses should endeavour to engage with outsiders through doorstep ministry. The main purpose of this door to door proselytizing, however, is not so much to promote religious cohesion but to attract prospective converts.[5] This monopoly over truth and tendency to dismiss all other religious doctrines as errant prevent exclusivists from partaking in interfaith initiatives. Unlike the religious inclusivists who feel they have something to learn from other faith communities, the exclusivists' main motivation for conversing with people who hold different beliefs is to win recruits.

It would be wrong to suggest that if ecumenical chaplaincy were to become more widespread, those who hold exclusive views will embrace religious cohesion in a more positive manner. There are two reasons why this is unlikely to happen. First, those who propound exclusive doctrines express their allegiance to a universal message that is impervious to social context. Exclusive movements, be they fundamentalist fringe groups or puritanical sects, are in pursuit of a theocratic mission across time and space regardless of their own popularity or of the (alleged) benefits of religious unity. It is this conviction that theirs is the *only* version of truth, accompanied by the certainty of their own salvation that prevents exclusivists from entering into faith partnerships. The second reason is more concerned with social change than with theological validity. Those with an exclusive outlook argue that it is *because* the world has become so amorphous that religious truth is now lost and that God's purpose for humanity has been obscured. According to this view, divine revelation has been shadowed by individualistic ideologies, material wealth and the pursuit of power, all of which have resulted in anxiety and uncertainty. In the West, religious exclusivity can be seen as an escape from intellectual mayhem and from a world on the brink of chaos, while in less economically developed parts of the world, it is a response to deprivation and to the absence of strong leadership. Whatever the analysis and whatever form these movements take, religious exclusivity and religious cohesion are, it seems, incompatible.

SECULAR INTEGRATIONISTS

It would be a mistake to assume that people with secular views are unable to recognize that faith communities can make a positive contribution to public life. Religious scepticism is complex and multi-faceted and its relationship with religiosity often simplified. Non-believers constitute a hugely heterogeneous group whose attitudes towards religion are shaped by a number of social and psychological factors. Strange as it might seem, secular thinkers may be more willing to partake in faith-oriented initiatives than members of some religious organizations; certainly more so than those who adopt an exclusive outlook.

Secular integrationists are people for whom integration and social well-being are important features of a liberal democracy. Though they are not themselves people of faith, secular integrationists respect the rights of others to hold religious beliefs without prejudice. The two general riders that they add to this are: first, that faith communities should avoid proselytizing (based clearly on the principle that religious beliefs are essentially a private matter) and secondly, that faith leaders should seek the consent of participants when facilitating religious activities. There is, of course, a whole philosophy about the relationship between religious practices and human rights (particularly where peripheral and/or vulnerable groups are concerned), and there is no agreement on the point at which the former could be said to impinge on the latter. Suffice to suggest that every scenario is unique and must be judged on its own merits.

Though they are people who hold ethical rather than religious values, not all secular integrationists espouse the same degree of scepticism. The extent to which they support or reject religious initiatives depends on a large number of factors; some personal, some environmental. The interviewees included here were unanimous in their view that people should be allowed to practice their faith freely and that religious groups had a right to be heard.

Some of these secular integrationists expressed a willingness to work with faith partnerships in promoting social justice and a small number were even prepared to attend interfaith events that promoted community cohesion. The following comments demonstrate the high levels of religious tolerance among four of these young people:

There are people who are religious and you have to understand that. I mean, my grandma doesn't go to church, but she sends them money and I think that's a good thing cos they help her when she needs it. People who are strong in their faith can support other people and do good things for Burnley. I'm friends with a lot of them. (White male atheist aged 25 years)

Some people are scared of faith cos they don't know what it is and they back off. We do different things at our youth club related to diversity and this can include faith; but if you preach to people you'll burn them off. Younger people are not into faith now cos times have changed. A lot of younger people have never known it. Don't get me wrong, some people do live by religion and that's what they need. (White female agnostic aged 22 years)

I've got friends outside work who are Muslims. I don't see them daily, but I do see them weekly. When I first went to secondary school, it was mainly White; but by the time I was in Year 9, it was becoming increasingly Muslim and that didn't bother me at all cos I live in a mixed area . . . faith is something a lot of people look up to. A lot of the things people do is for their faith and some people need that in their lives and you've got to respect that. I think there's a fine line between culture and faith, and even though I'm not a person of faith, I know it's important to some people. (White female atheist aged 23 years)

I work in a primary school where there are a lot of Asian kids and I always take part in Eid and Christmas festivals. I even fasted once during Ramadan for a bit of a joke cos my Muslim mates told me I'd never be able to do it! Everyone has something good to offer whatever faith or ethnic group they belong to. It's a lot to do with not knowing. In some schools in Burnley, like the Catholic schools, for example, there are still no Asians;

so some children are going through their whole school lives without any integration and I think that's terrible. A lot of the kids at the school where I work take part in the Bridge project and that's faith-based. It's managing to bring children from different backgrounds together. We take the children on visits to Catholic churches, mosques and Hindu temples; but it boils down to finding things that the kids are interested in. (White male agnostic aged 24 years)

Despite their religious scepticism, these interviewees clearly recognized that religious beliefs were important to other people. Their comments support the view that healthy scepticism requires a willingness to listen to views that they, the religious sceptics, find unconvincing. Most were supportive of interfaith initiatives and all believed that faith communities could contribute to civic renewal by working together. Two of the interviewees expressed this succinctly:

I do have religious friends, but we don't talk about religion much. I've done some voluntary work with *Building Bridges Burnley,* and I've also done some work with the cubs. It doesn't matter to me whether you're a person of faith or not. Muslims do a lot for their community and so do Christians; but I think if Christians and Muslims worked together, they could do it a lot more. (White male agnostic aged 21 years)

I know they are places of worship, but why can't churches and mosques come together more? Different faiths should go and visit each other's places of worship and talk about their own faith, and faith communities should welcome each other and encourage each other to do this. So many Christians know nothing, absolutely nothing about other faiths and they tend to believe everything that their own faith tells them . . . it's all about making an effort. (White male atheist aged 25 years)

All but one of the respondents were in favour of publicly funded interfaith projects, as long as participation was optional and that those involved in leading the initiatives made every effort to unite people from different faith backgrounds. This demonstrates an ability on the part of some secularists to leave aside their religious scepticism when being asked to comment on the strengths of religious cohesion. It should be borne in mind, however, that most of the respondents in this sub-group were employed either as youth and community officers or development workers in the public sector; hence, their support for cohesive projects was generally strong. It is also worth noting that more than half of these interviewees lived in mixed wards – an experience which no doubt accounted for their positive attitudes towards diversity. The following comments from a young woman in her twenties provide a good example:

> I remember when I lived in Bellington Road, I lived next door to Muslims and Indians and me and my mum and dad got on really well with them. They used to make us food and invite us to their weddings which we always went to; and then when my cousin was christened, they came to the christening. Anyway, all the White people who lived on the same street slowly started to move away and more and more Asians started to move in until eventually, we were the only White family left. But we got on with all of them . . . there wasn't one family that we didn't get on with . . . but then my mum and dad split up and we had to move because the house we lived in had three bedrooms and an attic and a cellar and it was too big for just me and my mum. (White female atheist aged 23 years)

While it would be impossible to introduce a policy of compulsory mixed settlement on the White and Asian communities of East Lancashire, it is highly likely that this young woman's appreciation of cultural and religious differences derived from her experience of living in an Asian-populated ward. This adds weight to the suggestion that racial and religious tolerance is improved when people experience personal contact with members of different religious and ethnic groups, though this will depend on how these opportunities present themselves in secular contexts. The key challenge for faith partnerships is to use these contexts to promote their mission and to galvanize the support of secular leaders. In divided communities, this is an onerous task that requires perseverance and commitment. School outreach provision, pastoral and community support in the voluntary sector and neighbourhood renewal projects provide some such opportunities. Despite their religious indifference, it is clear that the interviewees in this secular integrationist sub-group saw the potential for faith communities to work together and to unite with civic organizations in tackling segregation.

SECULAR AVERSIONISTS

The final sub-group – the secular aversionists – represents those who hold no religious beliefs and who reject the notion that faith communities can promote the public good. Secular aversionism holds no social class boundaries. Academics on the intellectual left of the political spectrum are as likely to berate religious initiatives as people from lower socio-economic strata, either because of their own (often negative) religious experiences or because they regard religion as a destructive force.

Secular aversionists are as resistant to interfaith projects as religious exclusivists, but for different reasons. The interviews and the school survey revealed evidence of religious antipathy among a sizable core of young people. The main forms in which this antipathy was expressed included an unwillingness to listen to people who held religious views, disdain for religious practices, disrespect for faith leaders and indifference to religious unity. The following comments from two young Burnley residents echo some of these views:

I don't think the religions in this town have ever really mixed until recently, but even if they do, it'll never work . . . People like me just aren't interested. We don't want to know. If people started coming preaching to me, I'd tell em to p*** off. The power of the mind of non-religious people is too strong. People of no faith live their own lives and have their own things to worry about and that's all they're interested in. I've never believed in religion, even as a kid. (White male atheist aged 20 years)

I refuse to step foot in a church and if people get on the wrong side of me about religion, they regret it. It's all s*** in my eyes. Even at the age of about five, I can remember thinking to myself: 'What the hell's all this about?'; but at that age, you don't really have a choice. It was only in my teenage years that I finally turned round and told Christianity to kiss my butt! A lot of so-called religious people would rather see each other die than be friends. I mean, how can religions come together when most of England is only Christian and Muslim, and even that's dying out? (White male atheist aged 19 years)

The religious aversion expressed by these two interviewees presents no small challenge for faith communities. Unlike the secular integrationists who could at least see the potential for faith groups to contribute to the public good, these respondents dismissed all such possibility, believing instead that all organized religion was divisive and that any attempt by faith partnerships to tackle segregation was bound to fail. Although it would have taken a different kind of investigation than this one to explore the reasons for these attitudes, it is worth noting that both these young men had lived in Burnley all their lives and were unemployed at the time of the interviews. It is likely, therefore, that despite their rejection of religious beliefs in childhood, their experiences of growing up in a segregated town that offered few prospects and where expectations among a large number of young people were low had had a strong impact on their cognitive development and general world view.

The Year 10 questionnaire survey also unearthed evidence of religious adversity. These attitudes were far more pronounced among White non-Christian pupils than any other group. In a school with a majority-White population, only 21 per cent of the respondents believed that pupils in their own school showed respect for each other's religious beliefs and only 50 per cent expressed a willingness to listen to other people's religious views. Even more discouraging was the fact that only 29 per cent of the pupils in this school stated that they would like to see different faith communities working together.[6] These high levels of intolerance pose a considerable challenge to those who are keen to encourage young people to value religious diversity and to recognize that religious beliefs are important to many British citizens.

Needless to say, it is difficult for faith partnerships to engage with young people who express unequivocal religious resistance. Such attitudes do not bode well for initiatives that aim to unite all sections of society and that are working hard to achieve community cohesion. Faith groups will need to find innovative ways of reaching youngsters who hold entrenched secular views and whose respect for ethnic, cultural and religious diversity has been marred by social and political disaffection.

The religious attitudes of school pupils: a comparative analysis

The Year 10 questionnaire survey produced some of the most illuminating data on the religious attitudes among teenagers in East Lancashire that I have ever seen. The purpose of the survey was to explore the relationship between school composition and religious tolerance. The questionnaire contained 36 (mainly closed-ended) questions, all of which were intended to elicit students' attitudes towards religious diversity, faith leadership, social integration and liberal democracy. The three schools selected (referred to below as Schools A, B and C) were similar in size, but very different in terms of their religious and ethnic group composition.[7]

School A (located in Burnley) was attended almost exclusively by White pupils from low-income families living in wards in which there were notoriously high levels of crime and anti-social behaviour. Despite its unequivocal anti-racist/anti-bullying policy, this was a school in which racist attitudes among pupils were allegedly widespread and where there was a woeful lack appreciation for cultural diversity. School B was located in a more affluent location in the comparative town of Blackburn, but attracted students from similar socio-economic backgrounds to School A. Unlike School A, however, approximately 96 per cent of School B students were of Pakistani or Indian heritage – a consequence both of gradual Asian settlement in the area since the 1960s and of subsequent White flight. Of the three schools surveyed, this school drew pupils from the widest geographical area, many of whom travelled to school on public transport. School C (also in Blackburn) was in a similar location to School B and recruited pupils from wards with greater or lesser degrees of deprivation. This school was chosen because of its ethnic mix (73 per cent of the pupils were White British while the remaining 27 per cent were of Asian heritage) which made for a potentially interesting analysis of young people's attitudes. With the exception of only one other school (a school in

Burnley which recruited equal numbers of pupils from both ethnic groups, but which had to be rejected because of its single-sex status), this school had the largest number of pupils from different religious and ethnic backgrounds sharing the same social space. It is in a school like this that one might expect to find fairly high levels of interaction and integration.

The socio-economic profiles of the pupils were similar in all three schools. In School A, less than 8 per cent of the pupils had at least one parent in a professional or semi-professional occupation. In Schools B and C, the figures were 10 and 11 per cent, respectively. These professional groups included teaching, nursing and college lecturing. Of the more senior professions, one parent was a dentist, one was an architect, two were probation officers, two were accountants and three were police officers. The majority non-professional occupations varied, but surprisingly few parents – only around 15 per cent of the total sample – were employed in craft-based industries such as building, engineering, technological assemblance, electronics and car maintenance. Most of the parents were employed as retail assistants and supervisors, support workers, lower grade clerical assistants, care assistants, cleaners, dinner ladies, bar workers and factory workers. Around 20 per cent of the parents were newsagents, sub-post officers, taxi drivers and landlords, while almost one-third of the mothers of pupils of Asian heritage were housewives. Of the parents who were employed, it was unclear how many worked on a part-time basis and/or how many were divorcees with children under school age. None the less, the similar socio-economic backgrounds of the pupils across all three schools made for an interesting comparative analysis.

FAITH COMMUNITY LEADERSHIP
AND OTHER SOURCES OF INFLUENCE

The survey findings showed that religious convictions varied considerably between the pupils, but it was the results of Schools A and B that were the most illuminating. In School A, only 19 per cent of the Year 10 population believed in God and only 16 per cent had been exposed to religious influences by parents or other relatives. In School B, the results were 97 and 96 per cent, respectively.

Perhaps not surprisingly, regular religious worship (prayer and mosque attendance) and the observance of religious rules in daily life were more evident in School B than in either of the other two schools.

The relationship between religious conviction and church/mosque attendance was consistent in Schools A and B. In School B, over 81 per cent of the Year 10 population attended mosque at least once a week (representing most of the Muslims in the year group) compared with only 8 per cent of weekly church attendees in School A. One of the most significant findings, however, was that over one quarter of the School B pupils claimed that the mosque was the most important influence in their lives while none of the pupils in School A attributed this degree of influence to a church. The greatest influence in the lives of all the pupils was the home (45, 41 and 33 per cent for Schools A, B and C, respectively), though for School A pupils, friends were considered equally influential. Attitudes towards religious leadership were also quite revealing with over 43 per cent of School B pupils giving greatest deference to a religious leader compared with only 2 per cent of pupils in School A and 11 per cent in School C. There was clearly some contradictory evidence here among School B pupils over whether relatives were more influential than religious leaders.

The survey results confirmed that exposure to religious activities outside school had a bearing on attitudes towards faith leaders. The high frequency of mosque attendance among School B pupils and their extensive religious socialization had a strong influence on how they viewed religious clerics. It is also worth noting that 68 per cent of the School B pupils were able to name an imam compared with only 41 per cent of School A pupils who were able to name a Christian minister (attributable, most likely, to the fact that the local Anglican priest was a regular school visitor). While there was no doubting the high degree of deference shown to religious leaders by School B pupils, further research would be required to explore exactly what kind of religious messages were being conveyed both in the home and in the mosque.

There were a number of factors which helped to explain the relatively weak influence of religious leaders in the lives of the pupils in School A, the most significant of which were the level of general interest in religion and the importance attached to its status. Only 13 per cent of these pupils claimed to be either very interested or interested in religion, 19 per cent claimed to be a little interested and 68 per cent found it boring (compared with 91, 8 and 1 per cent, respectively for School B). At the same time, 59 per cent of School A pupils thought that religion was unimportant or did not care and, as already stated, only 50 per cent were either very willing or reasonably willing to listen to other people's religious views compared with figures of 10 and 86 per cent, respectively for School B.

MONO- AND DUAL-CULTURAL EDUCATION
WITH PARTICULAR REFERENCE TO RELIGION

Given the complexity of measuring religious attitudes and the large number of influences both in and outside education, it is difficult to establish the extent to which schools promote or impair religious tolerance. The findings from this survey confirm that over one quarter of the School A pupils believed that their school had not helped them to understand different religious beliefs compared with only 5 per cent of the pupils in School B and 12 per cent in School C. The school, however, was considered by far the most common provider of knowledge of different religious faiths of any institution among all three cohorts of pupils surveyed. This would suggest that even where levels of religious indifference are high, community schools are able to raise the profile of religion and in so doing, promote a concept of religious unity. What is less clear is whether this is best achieved in mixed or mono-cultural schools.

The fact that only 8 per cent of pupils in School A and 12 per cent of pupils in School C expressed an interest in learning more about other people's religious beliefs (compared with 42 per cent in School B) suggests that it is those pupils who had internalized a religious code who were most likely to recognize the importance of understanding different religious beliefs. This highlights not only the potential for faith cohesion initiatives in schools, but the challenge facing *all* teachers in encouraging pupils to recognize the value of religious understanding, even (or especially) where religious conviction is weak.

The religious attitudes of the pupils were also tested in a question concerning whether or not Christianity and Islam taught the same ways to be a good person. Only 40 per cent of the School A pupils believed this to be the case while 21 per cent said they did not know and 28 per cent said they did not care. In contrast, the responses of the School B pupils to the same question were 83, 3 and 1 per cent, respectively. School C was more comparable to School A than to School B with 41 per cent of the pupils responding in the affirmative, 17 per cent saying they did not know and 26 per cent saying they did not care.[8] This would suggest that although schools are key providers of religious knowledge, it is those pupils with the strongest religious beliefs who are most likely to digest the information and to reflect seriously on what they are being taught in classrooms. At present, it is uncertain whether dual-cultural schools would be any more successful in capturing the interest of religiously indifferent pupils in segregated towns than mono-cultural schools.

The end of integration?

The above findings cast doubt on the so-called 'end of integration' thesis. According to this thesis, ethnic communities in Britain are ceasing to be concerned about integrating with the 'host' society and are instead strengthening their ties with their ethnic and national homelands.[9] The survey questions which attempted to address this issue revolved around mixing with others, the nature of out of school activities, attitudes towards race and ethnicity, views on religious cohesion, attachment to place of origin and, most important of all, allegiance to common values.

It was clear from the questionnaire data that while the pupils from all three schools mixed with young people from other parts of their town on a regular basis, the contexts in which these interactions took place varied. For the pupils in Schools A and C, the streets provided the most common arena for mixing with people their own age while for School B pupils, it was sports centres, playing fields and parks. While it would have taken a different survey to ascertain the extent to which sporting activities across the two towns united young people from different social and cultural backgrounds, there was good reason to believe that sports centres provided an appropriate arena (and indeed one of the safest spaces) for social interaction. The greatest challenge, it seemed, was that of how to entice young people away from street corners and into more structured, community-based activities that would make this interaction possible.

Undoubtedly the most disturbing finding of the survey resulted from a question concerning race.[10] Approximately three quarters of the pupils from all three schools believed that there were different races, but it was in School A that the highest percentage of pupils believed that one race was superior to another (almost 30 per cent of the year group believed this to be the case compared with 11.3 per cent in School B and 18.5 per cent in School C). The greater degree of racial tolerance in an overwhelmingly Asian/ Muslim populated school calls into question the common sense assumption that mixed schools represent the most tolerant environments. The results of this survey show that it was the Asian/ Muslim pupils in both the mixed and the mono-cultural schools who were, in fact, the most tolerant of all. The key question is whether White non-Muslim pupils who attend mixed schools demonstrate a greater degree of religious and ethnic tolerance than their counterparts in mono-cultural schools.

Attitudes towards religious cohesion produced data consistent with those above. The fact that only 29 per cent of the pupils in School A were in favour of different faith communities working together compared with 76 per cent of School B pupils highlights the need to find more secular ways of promoting integration. School C pupils occupied the middle ground with 34 per cent supporting religious unity, 15 per cent opposing it and the remaining 51 per cent expressing either uncertainty or indifference. Further analysis confirmed that only 3 per cent of the Muslim pupils from across all three schools were opposed to the formation of faith partnerships compared with 26 per cent of Christians and 16 per cent of those with no religious affiliation. These findings suggest that levels of religious tolerance and the willingness to mix with people from other religious groups were, among Muslim pupils, exceptionally high.

Despite the negative impact of events such as 9/11 and 7/7 on ethnic relations in the UK, the survey confirmed without doubt that Year 10 Muslim pupils living in East Lancashire were comfortable with their Islamic beliefs and, by the criteria adopted in this investigation, well integrated. While 56 per cent of the Muslim pupils in School B and 62 per cent in School C expressed strong attachment to their ancestral homelands, the overwhelming majority supported liberal democratic values such as showing respect for others regardless of social class, ethnicity, gender and religion, freedom of speech even if it caused offence, being friendly to people from other religious and/or ethnic groups, tolerating those with different views and, most interesting of all, showing loyalty to the UK. Perhaps the most surprising result was that around 90 per cent of the Muslim pupils in School B and 95 per cent in School C believed in the value of finding one's own way in life rather than depending on others. This suggests that while Islam places great emphasis on surrendering to the will of Allah, an increasing number of young Muslims are finding their own ways of embracing self-reliance and of incorporating this into their religious identities. There would be much mileage to be gained from testing the generalizability of these data in other Muslim communities both locally and nationally.

While the attitudes of the Muslim pupils to questions of liberal democracy were largely positive, the responses of the majority White pupils in School A had negative implications for community relations. Almost one half of the School A pupils felt that respecting others regardless of gender and religion was unimportant and almost one third felt the same way about cultivating friendships with people from different religious and ethnic backgrounds. Around 66 per cent of these pupils believed in free religious and political speech even if it caused offence and almost one quarter felt that it was unimportant to show tolerance to those with different views. The responses of these School A pupils to the values of self-reliance (approximately 95 per cent felt this to be important or fairly important) and showing loyalty to the UK (supported by around 87 per cent) were comparable to those of the majority Muslim pupils in School B and the smaller number of Muslims in School C. Despite the consensus between the Muslim and the non-Muslim pupils on these issues of free speech, national loyalty and self-reliance, the much higher levels of intolerance among the School A pupils towards people from different religious and ethnic groups along with their widespread belief in racial superiority reflected an insular, parochial outlook and an illiberal social and cultural perspective.

Implications for the future

There is sufficient evidence both from the in-depth interviews and the school survey to suggest that although the different faith and ethnic communities of Burnley and Blackburn manage to live amicably together most of the time, these are largely segregated towns in which social interaction is tenuous and unsustained. This segregation manifests itself in housing (with the largest percentage of Asian residents concentrated in two or three of the most deprived wards), in school composition and in a range of other social and cultural activities. It is worth noting, however, that a number of initiatives were launched in both towns between 2001 and 2007 including annual cultural events, neighbourhood renewal schemes, urban regeneration programmes, interfaith projects and, perhaps most significant of all, the restructuring of secondary education; all of which had the potential to improve integration and to challenge some of the negative perceptions that the main faith and ethnic communities held of each other. My research findings reveal that the most negative of these attitudes tended to take root within parochial, mono-cultural communities in which awareness and understanding of other cultural perspectives were limited and based, for the most part, on deeply internalized prejudices.

There is every reason to believe that with enough will and financial support, teachers, religious leaders and youth workers can help remove some of these barriers to community cohesion. The so-called privatization of religious belief and observance is, paradoxically, being accompanied by renewed interest in the influence of religion on public life and social policy. In Burnley, there were several levels on which the two main religious groups were beginning to operate – on civic renewal steering committees, in local network organizations, in schools and in the planning of public events. Moreover, the 40 interviews with young adults elicited a relatively high degree of religious tolerance, even among those who did not hold religious beliefs. While this was only a small number of interviewees and not, therefore, representative of the Burnley borough, it should be emphasized that the participants were selected from a wide range of secular organizations and voluntary groups in and around the town. This suggests that there is considerable scope for community-oriented schemes to involve faith partnerships.

The interview data revealed variations in attitudes within faith and secular communities as well as between them. The typology presented in this chapter is an attempt to frame some of these attitudes and to provide a model that may be of use to those working with religious groups in the future. It is important to mention, however, that this typology has been constructed only from the data collected during this investigation and should not be regarded as a blueprint for interfaith dialogue. What it does demonstrate is the complexity of people's willingness to partake in religious cohesion initiatives and the difficulties involved in formulating strategies that reflect the mission of faith partnerships. As far as the facilitation of interfaith projects is concerned, the diversity of religious attitudes discussed in this section presents teachers, religious leaders and project facilitators with the problem of who to include in a particular initiative as well as how to include them. Those working in secular contexts, on the other hand, may find that there is much to be gained from including people of faith in the community cohesion agenda in the hope that this will reflect social diversity and strengthen the capacity of voluntary provision.

From the very beginning of my research, it was clear that the attempts of faith communities to tackle social segregation must, at some point, involve engaging with young people of school age, for it is only by exploring the religious attitudes of school pupils that the potential of future initiatives can be established. If conducted with appropriate methodological rigour, research of this kind can be used to ascertain the form that these initiatives might take and how they could be implemented. The Year 10 survey suggests that the BNP in Burnley had had a strong influence on local people in 2006 (reflected in the fact that the party had control of six seats) and that there were few signs of this diminishing. It is highly likely that the several thousand BNP voters representing approximately 10 per cent of the town's May 2005 electorate were themselves parents of some of the pupils who took part in the survey. It is these pupils who are in receipt of mixed messages and who present the biggest challenge to teachers responsible for the delivery of Citizenship and Religious Education. Equally challenging is the question of what inroads, if any, faith partnerships can make into this difficult territory.

By far the greatest concern that the survey results present and one that continues to have far-reaching implications for education policy is the fragility of the White British identity. Paradoxically, it is the efforts of teachers to promote cultural diversity in segregated towns (verified by several teachers themselves during the course of my investigation) that have been met by the resistance of parents who object to multicultural education on the grounds that it undermines Britishness.[11] It is the cumulative effect of myths and stereotypes, negative perceptions of cultural diversity and fundamental fear of difference that teachers, outreach workers and community leaders must make every effort to combat. This calls for the exploration of new definitions of Britishness and the need to help those who define their identities in exclusive, nationalistic terms to channel their ideas into something more holistic.

The educational research which I carried out alongside the Year 10 survey unearthed the very different ways in which high schools in East Lancashire were approaching Citizenship Education. It was abundantly clear that provision was patchy between institutions and that in some cases, teachers were paying little other than lip service to this relatively new area of the curriculum. My research findings did, however, confirm that project-based initiatives and/or cultural events worked far better than didactic classroom delivery. Needless to say, teachers need to be given time to prepare innovate lessons and to work together to produce an experiential curriculum model that will achieve the objectives set out by the QCA. Any future educational research would do well to explore the possible contribution that faith communities might make to the curriculum and to evaluate some of the practices currently deemed successful.

There is much more work to be done on the relationship between the religious and ethnic group composition of schools and the formation of social attitudes. The data I have presented in this chapter about the extent to which majority and minority ethnic groups are prepared to embrace difference. The Year 10 survey data suggests that Muslim students of Asian heritage living in segregated English towns may be more willing than their White Christian and non-Christian counterparts to accept social diversity without feeling that their identities are being threatened. It should be borne in mind, however, that these conclusions were only drawn from a questionnaire survey carried out among the pupils of one year group and from a series of mainly closed-ended questions. The fact that this was only a two year investigation meant that longitudinal validity was impossible to achieve. What the survey does highlight, however, is the need for more comparative research between mono-cultural, dual-cultural and multicultural schools (both faith and non-faith) across a wide range of educational sectors. It is only through research of this kind that investigators will be able to identify the different ways in which educational providers can help to create a more integrated society.

Notes

1 For a description of the two Burnley wards in which most of the fieldwork was conducted, see Appendix 4.

2 Non-Government Organizations.

3 It is important here to consider the extent to which perceptions of ethnicity are influenced by perceptions of faith.

4 A reflection, perhaps, of the fact that Islam is a less diverse system of belief than Christianity.

5 For a more detailed analysis of the proselytizing activities of the Jehovah's Witnesses, see Holden 2002a and 2002b.

6 Of the remainder, 22 per cent said they would not, 24 per cent said they did not know and 25 per cent said they did not care.

7 The data were useful, therefore, for comparative purposes.

8 The reason these figures do not total 100 per cent is because a small number of pupils selected other options such as 'in some ways', 'not in very many ways' and 'do not understand the question'.

9 Burdsey (2006) describes how young British Asians are able to express both their cultural heritage *and* the permanency of their settlement in Britain through sporting affiliations.

10 The concept of race was used intentionally since it was felt that students of school age would understand it more easily than the term *ethnicity*.

11 Of undoubted significance here are the results of a local piece of research carried out by Burnley Borough Council immediately after the 2001 disturbances which revealed widespread resentment among White residents towards the town's Asian community over the allocation of public resources and the effects of post-war immigration on house prices.

3. Religious cohesion in schools and colleges

The education system is one of many institutions in the UK able to promote religious and cultural diversity. Since educational provision is compulsory for all children (with a small number of exceptions) between the ages of 4 and 16 years, the opportunities for schools to raise awareness of religious issues are endless. A school is an environment not only where learning takes place, but where children spend long periods of time together. Whatever the nature of the curriculum, be it nationally or independently formulated, religious knowledge is likely to form a lasting impression, not only because this knowledge is delivered as part of the national curriculum (as in the case of Religious Education and Religious Studies), but because it is imparted at a time when the values and attitudes of young people are taking root. Although there is nothing deterministic about the effects of classroom learning (children are, after all, exposed to a wide range of influences outside education), few would doubt its potential to make a difference. In times of conflict, the need to cultivate positive community relations in multicultural towns and cities is imperative.

Since 9/11, the increasingly negative perceptions of Muslims both at home and abroad have added a religious dimension to international relations. In areas of the UK where people are divided along ethnic lines and where religious convictions vary between different groups, the interplay between national, religious and ethnic membership manifests itself in a variety of social contexts. The purpose of this chapter is to highlight the opportunities for engendering respect for religious differences in schools and colleges and to describe some of the ways in which Christian–Muslim unity can be promoted by teachers, lecturers and outreach workers.

Needs and opportunities

Until quite recently, there have been few sustained attempts to address cohesion issues through the school curriculum. The last three decades of equal opportunities legislation have brought about some significant changes in employment, housing and a range of other public services. Welcome though these changes have been, they do not, in themselves, produce social unity and in some instances, they may even detract from it. A genuine acceptance of and respect for cultural difference is an attitudinal requisite that can only be advanced through awareness-raising. This is something to which educational establishments can make a contribution.

In the 1960s and 1970s, examination syllabuses rarely made reference to non-western religion or culture, despite the post-war settlement of large numbers of migrants from the Caribbean, the West Indies and the Asian sub-continent. Moreover, the multicultural initiatives launched in the 1980s (at a time, incidentally, of growing concern about the poor educational performance of children from BME communities) were denigrated by the Thatcher government as left-wing and dissident.[1] But times have changed and the need to recognize the value of social diversity has made its way back on to the political agenda. In the last decade or so, there have been renewed attempts to achieve this through the national curriculum, though provision in many local authorities remains patchy and underdeveloped. In East Lancashire, most schools and colleges have made a conscious effort to include non-Anglo-Saxon perspectives in their curricula and to help young people to respect other cultures and creeds. If the results of my research in Burnley and Blackburn reflect those of elsewhere, the inclusion of religious cohesion activities can be of considerable benefit to the British education system. The time has come to revisit the principles of previous educational models that aimed to promote tolerance and understanding, whatever new term we might use to advance these principles in the future.

The issue of how the education system should facilitate social integration remains a bone of contention. At present, there is little consensus about what form this should take and there are no standard benchmarks by which to measure its success. In contrast with both the *assimilationist* model (the dominant model in many early studies of ethnicity which argued for cultural unification) and the *multicultural* model (that is, an approach which sought to protect cultural distinctiveness), the present model is one that might be described as *integrationist* – an approach that extols unity *and* diversity at one and the same time.[2] Whatever credence people might give to these different models, teachers and head teachers continue to disagree about where in the school/college curriculum multicultural issues might be addressed and whether religious diversity should be included. Furthermore, concepts such as 'religion', 'faith' and 'spirituality' mean different things to different people. While few parents object to their children learning about different religious traditions as part of a nationally agreed RE syllabus,[3] the inclusion of anything exceeding a modest amount of multifaith, multicultural education would be likely to provoke a negative reaction. At the time of my research, a small number of parents in Burnley and Blackburn continued to object to their children partaking in multicultural festivals or visiting different places of worship. This calls for a debate about what exactly an integrationist curriculum should contain and whether non-Western cultures should receive more attention than at present. It is to these complex and controversial issues that most schools and colleges are left to find their own solutions.

There can be little doubt that the bipolar ethnic and religious landscape of East Lancashire and the spatially segregated areas in which people continue to live lend themselves to an inclusive curriculum model. Such a model is not one that advocates the need for young people to abandon their own beliefs and ways of life in the interests of 'assimilation', but one that promotes the strengths of diversity through positive engagement. An approach of this kind requires commitment and skill, but it is not an impossible feat. Its success depends on the extent to which teachers, lecturers, outreach workers and other educational facilitators are genuine advocates of these objectives and whether, as individuals, they are suited to the task. Principals and head teachers who try to implement cross-school/college policies may be making a grave mistake.[4] While some academic subjects present opportunities for teachers to raise awareness of different cultural and religious traditions, the implementation of strategies that encourage religious unity requires an understanding of other ways of life that can only be acquired over lengthy periods of time. Chaplains, faith co-ordinators and representatives of interfaith groups are better able to attempt this than teachers and lecturers, not only because they are themselves people of faith, but because they are in regular contact with different faith communities.

Within the first 2 months of the investigation, I interviewed teachers and chaplains from eight high schools and from four colleges of Further Education (three of which were Sixth Forms). With the exception of the Further Education colleges, the interviews were conducted with Heads of Citizenship and/or Religious Education. The purpose of the interviews was to establish the religious and ethnic composition of the establishments and the amount of curriculum time devoted to religious issues. Several months later, a borough-wide workshop for these teachers and their colleagues was held at one of the Burnley high schools. The workshop was intended as an opportunity for teachers, outreach workers and other practitioners to share resources and to discuss some of the initiatives in which they were involved. The ultimate purpose of the exercise was to establish a consortium of educational practitioners in the East Lancashire area who were keen to exchange ideas about how religious cohesion could be included in the curriculum and to improve the provision in their own places of work.[5]

The initial interviews with teachers revealed that although provision varied between institutions, the range of activities aimed at promoting religious cohesion was narrow. The two Roman Catholic schools provided Christian chaplaincy services while the Further Education college had the remnants of a Christian and an Islamic Union. The Christian Union had held weekly meetings until the summer of 2005, but this had slipped into decline by the autumn with only two or three remaining members. The Islamic Society had had a more vibrant membership with around 15 Muslim students, but this too had dwindled as a result of a high number of the students involved in work placements. The fluidity of membership and general diminution of activity in both these Unions suggests that however strong the students' level of religious faith might have been, there were few opportunities for these two different groups to enter into dialogue or to share their beliefs in other ways. This scenario reflects the largely secular and fragmented nature of post-16 education.

Unlike the Further Education colleges, the eight high schools each provided religious worship as part of their statutory obligation.

Occasionally, representatives of the *Burnley Evangelical Schools Trust* (a small group of adult Christian volunteers) visited the schools to deliver assemblies. One assembly per week was scheduled for each year group in most of these schools, while in the two Roman Catholic schools, daily prayers were included in tutorial and registration periods. Priests and in-house chaplains played an active pastoral role in the Roman Catholic schools where chaplaincy teams also prepared the liturgy for feast day masses. Imams seldom made visits to any of the educational establishments other than the colleges of Further Education.

It was clear from the interviews that there was a strong concept of religious and ethnic diversity among local teachers. There were, it seemed, several reasons for this. First, the 2001 disturbances had alerted the biggest majority of public sector employees to the prospect of further civil unrest in northern England if some serious attempts to tackle segregation were not made. Between 2001 and 2007, teachers in East Lancashire had given considerable thought to how cohesion issues might be included in the curriculum and how this might help to improve relations across ethnic and religious divides. The second reason relates, in a rather sinister way, to the first. More than half the teachers I interviewed expressed concern about the number of children whose parents and other relatives were BNP voters and, in some cases, active members of the BNP itself. This presented teachers with the difficult task of having to challenge racist assumptions before they could address religious and ethnic diversity in a positive manner. Pupils who were exposed to these racist influences were in receipt of contradictory messages when they were away from school, giving rise to the old sociological debate about the effects of home background on young people's cognitive processes.[6] The final reason concerns the pupils themselves and their tendency, unwittingly or otherwise, to create segregated social spaces. Teachers employed in the two most ethnically mixed schools in the east of Burnley reported that while there was little evidence of racial tension within their schools, pupils tended to associate, both in and outside classrooms, with people from the same ethnic group. Despite these tendencies, some teachers were making an effort to emphasize the benefits of diversity through their own subject areas. Teachers of the Arts and Humanities, for example, were in a better position to promote integration than some of their colleagues because their subjects lent themselves to cultural and religious debates. Subjects such as Physics, Chemistry, Mathematics and Information Technology, on the other hand, tended to be delivered didactically and presented fewer opportunities for the advance of the integrationist curriculum model.

My research findings revealed significant differences in the ways in which religious cohesion was attempted in schools and colleges in these segregated East Lancashire towns. Secondary and post-16 education presented a wide range of opportunities for pupils to learn about each other's ethnic, national and cultural traditions and to acquire a positive concept of social diversity. Religious beliefs cannot be ignored in this endeavour since they are central to the identities of most BME groups living in the UK. For those with little or no religious faith (teachers as well as students), respect for religious communities is essential for cohesion, particularly in places where there is a history of civil tension. Equally, those for whom religious beliefs matter profoundly must recognize that the religious indifference of secular humanists, atheists and agnostics is also a fundamental human right in a western liberal democracy. If the UK is to maintain its reputation as a generally tolerant society, it is essential that future generations of young people value this legacy. If the seeds of intolerance are allowed to be sown and take root in childhood, the task of reversing the process in adulthood becomes infinitely more difficult. An education system that encourages young people to respect difference and at the same time, cherish their own cultural heritage will have much to offer to the growth and development of a modern pluralistic society. This is no mean feat; but in much the same way that prejudice is internalized (and few social scientists would refute the claim that prejudice *is* learnt behaviour), it needs to be systematically and rigorously challenged.

The remainder of this chapter focuses on three examples (doubtless there are others) of how respect for religious diversity can be promoted in secondary and post-16 education. These include: (1) opportunities presented by classroom teachers; (2) cross-school/college provision and (3) outreach support. Before I discuss these examples, however, the concept of religious cohesion and the way in which it has been used in this book need clarity. The approach I have adopted is a holistic one, premised on the view that people of all faith communities and none can contribute to discussions and activities that aid religious understanding. The opportunities for this are endless. While concepts such as 'faith', 'spirituality' and 'conviction' are as difficult as ever to define, the need for young people to respect religious differences within the context of rights, responsibilities and individual freedoms is essential. Like all educational initiatives, however, success depends not only on how the activities are presented, but on the willingness of students to listen.

FAITH COHESION AT SUBJECT LEVEL

The information collected during the investigation provided numerous examples of how the issue of religious cohesion can be included in the school or college curriculum. The examples in this and the next section have been culled from the materials circulated through the teachers' consortium. Since it would be impossible to describe all the strategies – curricular, extra-curricular, vocational and academic – prepared by these teachers, what follows is a description of activities that received the most positive feedback (substantiated in an evaluation survey) from students.

Religious Education (RE) is currently a core-curriculum subject in secondary schools, but there is some confusion about its objectives. Much of this confusion derives from the failure to distinguish between religious *knowledge* (the dissemination of which is the main purpose of Religious Education and Religious Studies) and *collective worship* – a statutory requirement in secondary education and Sixth Form colleges. The delivery of RE involves the exploration of issues such as the meaning of life (essentially a philosophical endeavour), the importance of faith to religious devotees, the similarities and differences between world faiths, the changing nature of religiosity in modern societies, the causes of religious conversion, the study of sacred writings, the effects of religious behaviour on local communities, the legal status of religious organizations, the national and international influence of religious leaders and much more. The extent and the depth of this content vary depending on the syllabus selected by the school/college and on the level of study.[7] Whatever the indicative content of the syllabus, Religious Education does not, contrary to popular myth, involve students partaking in religious rituals such as prayer and meditation. Nor is it concerned with proselytizing or fund-raising.[8]

Like many other academic subjects, Religious Education and Religious Studies present ample opportunities to raise awareness of the commonality of religious experience whatever the level of enquiry. Among the best examples are the study of pilgrimages and festivals and the analysis of sacred texts. The first example was one that was used widely in East Lancashire at the time of my research. By establishing the common purpose of visits to places such as Jerusalem, Mecca and Lourdes, a teacher of Religious Studies is able to adopt an integrated approach to the purpose of pilgrimages which should, if delivered in an appropriate manner, cultivate the empathetic skills of religious and non-religious students alike. Similarly, the study of religious festivals such as Eid and Christmas is an effective way of developing a student's understanding of celebration and of raising his/her awareness of different religious feasts throughout the year. The second example – the study of biblical and koranic texts – is a different matter since it concerns religious beliefs rather than practice. It is here that students can explore the similarities and differences between the Abrahamic religions and use this knowledge to discuss differences in doctrine. Textual investigation is a key RS activity in many schools and colleges in the UK, particularly at the more advanced levels of study. According to the teachers I interviewed, this presented one of the best opportunities for Christian and Muslim students to learn (perhaps for the first time) about the origin and evolution of their own and other religious traditions. Moreover, it allowed those from other faith communities and/or those with no faith to explore the foundation of monotheism and to reflect on their own existential perspectives. In more general terms, the benefit of an exercise of this nature is not so much to impart knowledge of sacred texts, but to equip young people with listening skills and to help them to present an informed argument. These skills lie at the heart of effective dialogue.

In addition to these teacher-led approaches, the voices of students themselves can also be used to impart knowledge of religious beliefs. While this was not, in my view, used to its full potential in East Lancashire, there were some good examples of student-centred learning that are worthy of consideration. In one school, pupils were asked to prepare a short presentation of their beliefs with power-point technology. The presentation included images of religious symbols, family photographs of weddings and christenings, pictures of religious buildings and audio–visual resources such as video and CD Rom. Although the purpose of the exercise was to develop skills of communication (using Religious Education as an example), it did, in fact, raise awareness of different religious perspectives. For pupils who seldom engage beyond their own cultural and religious boundaries, an activity such as this can achieve more than its primary objectives.

In post-16 education, programmes such as Health and Social Care, Humanities and the Social Sciences also present opportunities for raising religious awareness. In AS and A Level Sociology, for example, the study of religion appears as a discrete module on all the major syllabuses. In Burnley and Blackburn, the AQA specification was taught in all three post-16 centres and, in line with the national trend, Sociology was one of the most popular A Level subjects. Fortuitously, the subject recruited students from the two main faith and ethnic groups. In the religion module, the indicative content included sociological theories of religion, the classification of religious movements, the impact of secularization on modern societies, the influence of the mass media on religious attitudes and the impact of religious beliefs on the construction of gender and ethnic identities. Since these issues concern religion as a *social* phenomenon, they give rise to discussions about the importance of religious faith in people's lives. Although one of the main requirements of academic programmes such as these is that students express their views within the theoretical and conceptual framework of the syllabus, an innovative teacher of Sociology can use this material to encourage and facilitate religious dialogue.

Other sociological issues such as the veiling of women, the representation of religious issues by the mass media, the high frequency of church attendance among Britain's Black population, the resurgence of religious fundamentalism and the contribution of religious groups to issues such as marriage, divorce and homosexuality present students with an opportunity to talk about their own beliefs and to challenge myths and misconceptions. Two teachers with whom I spoke enthused about their success in raising awareness not just of religious beliefs, but of different cultures. In classroom discussions about religious dress codes, for example, Muslim students would explain the meaning of the hijab – an issue that could be used as a catalyst for a more controversial discussion about whether full facial veils should be worn in public places. In the Sixth Form in which these two teachers were employed, a sizable number of Muslim girls would often remove their headscarves on their way to college, sparking a debate between Muslim students themselves about whether the hijab was a cultural or a religious symbol.[9]

Marriage and divorce were also issues that provoked lively classroom discussions. Large numbers of young people experience first-hand the consequences of divorce in the UK, and although this is an event that pulls hard at the heart strings, a Sociology or Citizenship workshop is one forum in which the issue can be debated. For many faith communities, divorce is a moral issue (in some cases, a religious prohibition) and it is here that Christian and Muslim students can identify common ground. Equally, there are opportunities for advocates of divorce (that is, students for whom divorce signifies little other than a practical solution to an unhappy situation) to present their secular views. According to the teachers, students who challenged religious injunctions would make reference to the increase in divorce reflected in national statistics – a controversial argument that would lead to discussions about the sanctity of marriage and of why marriages so often fail.[10] One lesson plan, the content of which made reference to differences in role relationships between ethnic groups, included an exercise in which students were asked to distinguish between *arranged* and *forced* marriages – an issue which is a source of confusion among many non-Muslims and which Muslims argue presents a distorted picture of Islam. If facilitated skilfully, lessons of this nature can be used as a vehicle for religious dialogue and give students an insight into prohibitions that they had previously failed to understand.

Vocational education presents rather different opportunities for raising religious awareness than academic programmes. The essence of a vocational programme is that knowledge is acquired through student-centred learning – a defining characteristic of a National Vocational Qualification (NVQ).[11] Since much of this knowledge is skills-based, students spend some of their time in a place of work where they are required to produce a portfolio of evidence. For students who are assigned placements in the public sector, this evidence is obtained through employment duties (practical tasks, interaction with clients, general administration and so forth), which aim to harness interpersonal skills. Students on Health and Social Care programmes are often allocated placements in nurseries, hospitals, care homes or GP surgeries – settings that attract people from a wide range of ethnic and religious groups. It is in these public sector spaces that Health and Social Care students can acquire knowledge of different faith communities and there are now several NVQ modules that address, explicitly as well as implicitly, issues of religious identity. One example of a written assignment that was presented at the Burnley consortium concerned an investigation into why so few women of first-generation Asian heritage attend clinics for periodical cervical smear examinations. Since the college attracted a large number of Asian girls, this created an opportunity for interfaith, intercultural dialogue.

The study of ethics is central to health education and the issues that cause concern among religious groups are now well documented. It is only by allowing faith communities to explain their objections to practices such as embryonic research, abortion and euthanasia that different ethical perspectives can be fully understood. At university level, medical students now spend a small amount of their time studying legal and philosophical issues in order to develop an awareness of the relationship between religion, medicine and law. In the last three decades, health journals have given more attention to issues of medical practices and religious beliefs. At a much lower level of study, awareness of some of these issues can be raised through vocational programmes in schools and colleges. In two of the post-16 establishments in which my research was conducted, the wall displays in the Health and Social Care base rooms depicted visual images of practices that have come to be associated with particular religious groups. Coursework topics also demonstrated this, examples of which included studies of sacred drugs in Rastafarianism, the rejection of medical treatment among Christian Scientists, the blood taboo among Jehovah's Witnesses, the prohibition of alcohol among Muslims and the dietary laws of Sikhs, Hindus and Buddhists. While some of these issues present greater opportunities for religious discussions than others, they all provide good examples of how the beliefs of different religious communities can be addressed in further education.

To present a case for faith representation in every subject in a school or college would, of course, be an endless task, but it is worth commenting on two or three more examples. In History, the study of African slavery unearths historical and political events (exemplified also in African music) that help to contextualize the social status of second and subsequent generation Black British communities for whom religion (particularly Christianity) is an important part of identity. Drama, too, offers an effective way of raising religious awareness. Role-play is a powerful teaching strategy that can act as a vehicle for the expression of social and religious ideas. With appropriate management, teachers of Drama can use theatrical performances to present hard-hitting messages about the consequences of extreme nationalism, racism, anti-Semitism, Islamophobia and other social and political ideologies that breed fear and prejudice. More importantly, stage-based settings provide one of the best forums for challenging misconceptions of religious groups and for relaying the positive influences of religious faith in people's lives. In this respect, fictitious dialogue can be used both as an anti-prejudicial device and as a means of encouraging students from different backgrounds to respect each other's traditions. Literature (rather than essentially *English* Literature) complements History and Drama in this endeavour. Since the late-1980s, there has been a conscious attempt in the UK to introduce students to the work of non-western writers in the hope that this will provide new insights into the dynamics of power. Texts such as *The Color Purple, To Kill a Mocking Bird* and *Othello* (not forgetting the plethora of poems and anthologies of a large number of Black writers) have played an instrumental role in challenging the ethnocentric bias of previous English Literature syllabuses and in narrating the life experiences of oppressed groups.

It is clear from the examples contained in this section that if religious cohesion is to be advanced in the British education system, religious *empathy* must first be created. Although there is some reference to moral and spiritual development in most subject syllabuses, this seldom receives anything other than tokenistic attention from classroom teachers who are given precious little time to prepare innovative lessons. If there is one point that is worth reiterating, it is that religious knowledge, in all its guises, is essential for religious unity. Perhaps, therefore, it is time for *all* teachers, notwithstanding the constraints of examination sylla-buses, to give more thought to how they are presenting their subject material to their students and to consider whether they are making the best possible use of human and physical resources. At the same time, policy makers need to devise flexible curriculum models in order to ensure that students are given reasonable access to these opportunities and that teachers and lecturers receive the support they need to build on existing practice.

CROSS-SCHOOL/COLLEGE PROVISION

In addition to subject knowledge, a large amount of learning takes place through a *form* or *tutorial* system in almost every school and college in the UK. The main purpose of the tutorial system is to enable teaching staff to impart information that is not necessarily knowledge based, but which needs to be delivered if schools and colleges are to function effectively. Tutorial sessions (usually one or two periods of a weekly timetable) have always been used by teachers and lecturers to carry out administrative duties such as student registration, form filling, announcing messages from Senior Management, electing school representatives, distributing reports, monitoring performance, assisting students with action plans, reviewing achievement, collating feedback, following up absences, arranging learning support and a whole host of other responsibilities that fall outside the subject timetable. This system of administration has changed little since the early-1970s, save for the fact that more and more of its content is driven by government policy.

The quality of the tutorial system has come to be seen, along with examination results, as an indicator not only of a school or college's ability to meet targets, but of the student's educational experience. The efficiency with which tutors (the majority of whom are also subject teachers) carry out these tasks is, along with academic teaching, subject to the rigors of Ofsted. In post-16 education, tutorial periods are used for the delivery of non-examinable curriculum content and for general administration. Most colleges of Further Education in the UK offer academic *and* vocational programmes and at present, students tend to select one of these two pathways. Like the secondary school curriculum, some post-16 programmes provide better opportunities for debating religious issues than others. In the Arts, Humanities and Social Sciences, for example, religious perspectives can be introduced with little difficulty as demonstrated in the previous section. The natural sciences such as Physics, Chemistry, Biology, Maths, Computing, Electronics and Information Technology, on the other hand, present students with few opportunities to engage in religious discussions. The cross-college tutorial system can be a conduit for addressing this imbalance.

The second reason for including faith related issues in the tutorial programme relates more to the general philosophy (or 'mission') of schools and colleges themselves than to subject choice. Since the early-1990s, educational establishments in England and Wales have taken active measures to make their equal opportunities policies explicit and most now refer to social and cultural diversity in their mission statements. While schools and colleges have always had systems in place for dealing with anti-social behaviour such as bullying, racism and homophobia, the failure to address these issues through the curriculum has, in some cases, resulted in poor Ofsted grades and subsequent recommendations for improvement. Some post-16 establishments have attempted to avert these criticisms by using the tutorial system to address human rights issues such as prejudice, discrimination, freedom of speech and freedom of religious expression. In voluntary-aided establishments such as Roman Catholic and Anglican Sixth Form colleges, cultural and religious diversity are receiving renewed attention as a growing number of these institutions have become multicultural and multifaith.

Despite more government intervention in recent decades, Sixth Forms are still able to use their tutorial system as a forum for addressing cohesion issues. At the time of my research, two Sixth Form colleges in Blackburn (one Roman Catholic, the other Anglican) used faith oriented material in their tutorial programmes. As in most post-16 establishments, the tutorial systems in these two colleges were compulsory, which meant that every full-time student received tutorial support as part of their weekly timetable. The students spent an average of one and a half hours a week in tutorial periods, although some of the sessions were used for assemblies. As one would expect, the content of the tutorial programmes differed between the two centres and both reviewed their provision on an annual basis. Since it was the Roman Catholic rather than the Anglican Sixth Form that recruited the largest number of Muslim students (making it the most religiously diverse of the two centres), it is the Roman Catholic tutorial programme that will be considered here.

In the autumn of 2005, this Roman Catholic Sixth Form attracted over 1,300 students (almost half of whom were non-Catholic) from local feeder schools. Around 25 per cent of the student population were of Asian heritage – a reflection not only of the ethnic composition of the town, but of the fact that the college had taken active steps to market itself as a community establishment with a strong Christian identity. Despite its Christian constitution, this was, to all intents and purposes, a multi-faith/multicultural institution which was recruiting students from the town's two main faith communities at an impressive rate. It was surprising, therefore, to find little evidence of voluntary interaction either in or outside classrooms between Christian and Muslim (or in ethnic terms, White and Asian) students. While this was not something for which the staff could be held responsible, it seemed that the tutorial system provided the best opportunity for the college to promote its community ethos and to ensure that representative quotas of students from different ethnic and religious backgrounds were placed in the same tutor groups.

In this Sixth Form college, two discrete 45 minute periods per week were allocated to the delivery of the tutorial programme. At the beginning of the academic year, the students were presented with a handbook containing articles, illustrations, newspaper extracts, quiz sheets, debating questions and a whole host of other activities.[12] Despite the college's Christian mission, it was clear from these materials that the chaplaincy team had adopted a holistic, inclusive approach that reflected the cultural, ethnic and religious diversity of the catchment area. The introductory sections of the booklet highlighted the college's commitment to Christian values (rather than Christian *liturgy*) and in so doing, the tutors were able to impart the college's all-encompassing message of inclusion. By focusing on humanitarian principles rather than Roman Catholic doctrines, the aim of the programme was to encourage students to think about their own beliefs when considering their relationships with others. Although some of the activities centred on images of God, the non-liturgical themes of respect for religious difference, self-empowerment and cultural diversity meant that *all* students (including those with no religious faith) were able to participate in the workshops. On some occasions, the tutorial periods were used for central presentations (often in the form of a short film or role-play performance) and it was here that the ethical values of social justice, equality, dignity, integrity and respect for human rights were addressed. The purpose of these presentations was to introduce issues of faith to the whole year group in order to provide a backdrop for the following tutorial periods. Each tutor was then asked to facilitate a series of discussions with his or her tutor group.

Underpinning this tutorial programme is the recognition that while it is impossible to achieve a consensus of opinion on issues of cultural and religious diversity, there is much to be gained from exploring themes common to humanity. The college's emphasis on ethics rather than liturgy enabled the tutors to accommodate all manner of religious and non-religious perspectives. This reflective model can only work in curriculum areas that are free from prescriptive knowledge and/or in establishments where those in positions of leadership are not motivated by their own political and ideological agendas. While this may present some concerns to religious conservatives, there can be no doubt that a humanitarian approach is suited to a multifaith, multicultural society.

Though appropriate, tutorial systems are not the only way of engendering religious cohesion in schools and colleges. In 2002, the Labour government's introduction of *Citizenship Education* was an attempt to encourage school pupils to acquire a common sense of national identity and to provide them with skills that would help them on their journey into adulthood. This new concept signalled the government's concern with fostering positive social relations in a rapidly changing world. After much deliberation, the subject was introduced in August 2002 at Key Stages 2 and 3 and as an option in primary and junior education. At the same time, the government introduced a revised personal and health programme which became known as *Personal, Social and Health Education* (PSHE), the aim of which was to heighten young people's awareness of health risks and to improve their knowledge of sexuality, sexual relationships, sexually transmitted diseases and a number of other personal issues. Over the last two or three decades, provision of this nature has provoked a range of responses across the social and political spectrum. Traditionalists have long argued that sex education is likely to arouse the curiosity of young people and encourage promiscuity. The concern here is that increased knowledge of sex and drugs will exacerbate the social problems with which the authorities are already having to deal. Advocates of a more liberal perspective, on the other hand, defend what they see as a more responsible and realistic way forward in a high-risk, media-driven society in which peer pressures (propagated by wider structural influences and reinforced by young people themselves) are reaching unprecedented levels. In this respect, PSHE is an attempt to manage a changing youth culture which, without responsible intervention, may move in a direction that the traditionalists fear most.

The Citizenship Education programme had a rather different agenda. The aim here was to improve pupils' knowledge and understanding of Western democratic societies with a view to creating a positive sense of national identity. The Qualifications and Curriculum Authority (QCA) validated a large number of Citizenship modules for all four Key Stages despite the Government's decision to make the subject compulsory only in secondary schools. At Key Stages 1 and 2 (that is, in primary and junior education), the modules were intended to improve children's awareness of public services, the legal system and civil life, examples of which included knowledge of the police, the media, children's rights and human diversity. At Key Stages 3 and 4, these issues would be studied in more detail incorporating elements of law, sociology, social policy, economics, politics and basic principles of philosophy. It was also hoped that by the end of Key Stage 4, secondary school pupils would have an elementary grasp of global issues and of the workings of the European parliament. If taught conceptually and thematically, Citizenship Education can also address issues of religious cohesion.[13]

Between 2005 and 2006, the quality of Citizenship Education provision in Burnley varied significantly. The interviews with Heads of Citizenship revealed that by and large, the quality of the delivery depended on the general status that had been assigned to the subject within the school – a factor that was itself dictated by the suitability of the staff and the commitment of senior managers.[14] This echoes some of the main findings of the Annual Report of Her Majesty's Chief Inspector of Schools for 2004/5:

> the story of the development of citizenship so far is one of qualified success. It remains the case that it is less well established in the curriculum than other subjects, and less well taught: indeed, some critics have seized on this as a reason for wanting to step back . . . Pupils' achievement in citizenship remains uneven. In general, schools have sought to establish pupils' knowledge and understanding about becoming informed citizens through discussion and short written responses, sometimes collaborative, sometimes using worksheets. More in-depth work, investigation and reflection, with substantial written outcomes, are less common. In some cases, the standards of pupils' written work in citizenship are lower than those in other subjects.
> (OFSTED, October 2005 http://live.ofsted.gov.uk/publications/annualreport0405/4.2.3.html)

The report confirmed that although Citizenship Education was making progress in terms of its infrastructural development, most subject leaders were self-trained. This was offered as one of the reasons for the failure of many schools to devote sufficient attention to the learning outcomes of the subject and to how it should be assessed. In Burnley, the infancy of Citizenship Education was patently clear. In most of the high schools, it was mainly teachers of Humanities (most notably, English, History and Religious Studies specialists) who had been appointed as subject co-ordinators – a responsibility that had been imposed on them from their line managers and for which the majority felt ill-prepared. This resulted in significant differences in both the amount of time allocated to the subject and how it was delivered. In one school, the subject had been incorporated into the PSHE programme (a strategy which the co-ordinator claimed had been successful), while elsewhere, it was delivered as a discrete curriculum area. In another school, the Senior Management Team had taken the decision to deliver the subject through the tutorial system – a strategy which, according to the subject leader, had produced little success as some of the tutors were unfamiliar with citizenship concepts.[15] These differences in delivery suggest that while there is much justification for the inclusion of Citizenship Education in the secondary school curriculum, some serious attention needs to be given to the issue of delivery.[16]

Despite these difficulties, it would be unfair to suggest that the Burnley schools had not had some success in raising religious, cultural and ethnic awareness through their Citizenship programmes. In almost half the schools, for example, diversity events were planned during the summer term. There was one particular activity that is worthy of mention. The school concerned – a medium sized comprehensive – was located in a deprived part of the town and had an intake of predominantly White pupils. According to the Head of Religious Studies, racist attitudes were widespread among the pupils, many of whom demonstrated an alarming degree of intolerance of anything other than their own very narrow concept of English culture. This endemic nationalistic parochialism both in and outside the school provided the rationale for the introduction of an annual Cultural Awareness Day.

The first of these took place on the school site and was made compulsory for all year groups at Key Staged 3. The aim of the initiative was:

> to give students the opportunity to identify, investigate and celebrate their cultural heritage, encouraging them to value the contributions made to their society by people from diverse backgrounds. Better racial tolerance and qualities of citizenship are the desired outcomes.[17]

On the day of the event, pupils from the selected year groups (that is, Years 7, 8 and 9) followed their normal timetable and attended their usual classes. Their teachers, however, had been asked to prepare lessons that were devoid of English content and to work as a team in order to avoid duplication. Year 7 pupils were told that throughout the day, their lessons would involve the study of Asian cultures, Year 8 would receive an African oriented education and Year 9 would learn about Eastern Europe. Heads of Department were given the freedom to invite guest speakers from the local community to help with the event and to enliven the material. Teachers were also encouraged to make use of multicultural resources, visual aids, IT and interactive learning aids. At break time and during the lunch hour, Asian and African music was played in the refectory while the pupils dined on Indian food.

The day began with a whole-year group activity in which the pupils were divided into small groups and asked to consider human differences and similarities (gender, hair colour, eye colour, interests, dress and so forth). The pupils were then instructed to separate these similarities and differences into the categories of 'heredity' and 'personal choice', the aim of which was to highlight the distinction between biological and cultural influences. This exercise was followed by an activity in which the pupils made a list of all the foreign countries they had visited and of the souvenirs they had brought home with them. In this way, the school was encouraging the pupils to consider the various physical items that first generation minority groups living in the UK had brought with them from their birth lands and how these came to be passed on from one generation to the next. The list was then extended to include non-physical items such as music, language and religious beliefs, all of which constituted something that could be called a 'collective culture'. The aim of this exercise was to encourage the pupils to identify cultural similarities and differences between ethnic groups. These activities provided the preamble for the afternoon workshops.

In addition to the substantive issues, it was clear that the teachers had made every effort to ensure that different styles of learning (visual, non-visual and kinaesthetic) were reflected in the workshop tasks in order to maximize pupil participation. In Physical Education, for example (a subject that appeals largely to kinaesthetic learners), pupils from different year groups received lessons in karate and javelin throwing – activities that had been selected to represent South East Asia and Ancient Greece; while in Geography, power-point images of the French education system were used to capture the interest of visual learners. Among the many other activities (too many to mention here) were a Chinese musical recitation, a interactive computer game entitled *Life in an Indian Village*, mathematical exercises using non-western number bases, a crossword containing non-English lexicons, the design of a multicultural website, the preparation of an Italian meal, the production of a Russian folk dance and the creation of an African mural. Throughout the day, the pupils recorded their experiences on dummy passports which they used to gain entry into the various countries represented by different parts of the school. The passports were stamped by the teachers at the start of each lesson once the pupils had crossed the fictitious border. When the day drew to a close, the pupils were asked to complete evaluation questionnaires which were passed on to the Curriculum Management Team.

The examples I have presented in this section lend strong support for cross-curricular initiatives that help young people to recognize the strengths of social diversity. There is no reason why religious beliefs should not be included in this strategy. Like most other educational models, however, cross-curricular initiatives are unlikely to succeed without meticulous planning. Few would doubt that annual events such as cultural awareness days offer a refreshing change from conventional classroom teaching and that they boost student motivation, but they are little other than tokenistic if no attempt is made to embed their outcomes into everyday educational practice. This requires teachers to be mindful of their own ethnocentric and religious prejudices and to make a conscious effort to reflect in their teaching the composition of the local community. In the present climate, there is some call for schools and colleges to consider new ways of supporting the community cohesion agenda, of which Citizenship Education is one example.

My findings suggest that cross-curricular approaches are a useful way of promoting ethnic, cultural and religious unity. There are, however, some caveats that should not be ignored. The cross-school/college tutorial system has always been regarded as a vehicle for the dissemination of information and for the provision of pastoral support rather than a forum for the discussion of philosophical, cultural and religious issues. Worrying though it might be, many teachers and lecturers regard tutorial responsibilities as irksome and mundane and their willingness to contribute to what might crudely be described as an integration agenda will depend not only on the curriculum content but on the workload of the tutor. At present, it may be expecting too much of teachers (particularly Maths, Computing, Science and Technology specialists) to address cohesion issues through a cross-school/college tutorial system. The suggestion that religious cohesion should be incorporated into Citizenship Education is equally problematic. At the time of my research, all but a very small number of teachers felt au fait with citizenship themes and most were uneasy about facilitating discussions that required an understanding of sociological, cultural and religious concepts. All things considered, it seems that while the cross-curriculum model offers an effective means of broadening the educational horizons of students, the issue of how best to achieve this is, at present, unresolved.

OUTREACH PROVISION

One of the most pioneering approaches to religious cohesion in schools and colleges is that of educational outreach work. In East Lancashire, faith partnerships have, in recent years, taken their mission into a number of primary and secondary schools with the aim of nurturing religious empathy among children of different ages. Although this approach is in its infancy, the current evidence suggests that it can make a valuable contribution to community cohesion in multifaith, multicultural localities. The outreach strategies described in this section lend support to the contributory faith cohesion model which I presented in Chapter 1.

In 2002, several members of the *Bridge* team (a BBB sub-group with a responsibility for offering enrichment activities to children of primary school age) started to visit local schools on a weekly basis as part of their organizational mission. The team comprised several part-time salaried employees, all of whom were managed by a Youth Development Officer.[18] The team focused most of its attention on children from deprived socio-economic backgrounds, since it was only by supporting children at risk of educational underachievement and the subsequent problems to which this might give rise (anti-social behaviour, youth offending, social exclusion and so on), that it was able to attract funding. In the autumn of 2005, the team planned to extend its provision to high school pupils – a proposal that provided part of the rationale for the formation of the teachers' consortium.

The team's intention to enter secondary schools in Burnley in the autumn of 2006 was a worthy one, but from a logistical point of view, the timing could not have been worse. The fact that the whole of the secondary education was about to be restructured in the borough presented a hindrance to any further curriculum development, no matter how innovative the plans. Fortuitously, Building Bridges Pendle (BBP) – an interfaith group in the nearby town of Nelson – had been working in both primary and secondary schools since 2001 and its outreach provision for Year 6 and 7 pupils had attracted the interest of several stakeholders. The main aim of the BBP team was to present a combined religious and cultural unity programme to the whole year group of the schools in the hope of making a contribution to the borough's community cohesion plan. By the summer of 2002, the team had visited 24 schools in the towns of Nelson and Brierfield,[19] and by the end of the academic year 2003/4, more than 4,300 pupils had completed the workshops. Although BBB and BBP were active in different boroughs, their approaches were similar. Both groups were aware of each other's contributions to education and the two project leaders had met some months earlier to exchange resources. It was the BBP team, however, that had had the most experience of working in the secondary sector.

The BBP team comprised three outreach workers – a Muslim, a Christian and a Hindu. In the event of absence, the team leader would request the input of other BBP members in order to ensure equal faith representation and to continue the tradition of a team-based approach. The triumvirate composition of the team reflected the religious diversity of the borough (although Christians and Muslims were by far and away the dominant faith groups) and the three members sought to convey to the pupils some of the ways in which people from different religious traditions could identify common ground. The representatives themselves came from different occupational backgrounds, but all were experienced in working with young people in the statutory and voluntary sectors. The team hoped that by matching the biographical profiles of its volunteers to the religious and ethnic membership of the local population, it would be able to address some important community relations issues in the Pendle area and give the workshops a more meaningful context. From the pupils' perspective, the opportunity to listen to outside speakers who were themselves local residents and who had no official connection with the school helped boost the status of the programme and gave a novel insight into some of the events that had taken place in the borough.[20]

The BBP programme comprised six consecutive weekly workshops, each lasting for one hour. These workshops reflected the guidelines for the delivery of PSHE and Citizenship Education and contained implicit and explicit interfaith elements. Throughout the period of their visits, the team sought to provide children with an opportunity to discuss controversial local and global issues in the safety of their school environment. If delivered successfully, the team believed that the programme would lead school pupils to a better understanding of diversity and of how this diversity had shaped modern Britain. The following excerpt from the BBP education mission statement demonstrates the team's attempt to link the programme to other areas of the national curriculum:

> The interfaith team carries the interfaith thread through all the PSHE/Citizenship work in schools. The interfaith team will ensure that social behaviour is related back to the interfaith perspective at regular intervals. Where there is sensitivity and conflict in faith matters, the team will propose alternative faith standpoints in a neutral manner, leaving the individual student to make their own commitments or solutions, using an inter-faith, non-faith, or faith tool . . . The presence of interfaith teams clearly coming from different faith traditions, and patently coming from outside a school culture is a major and unique strength. The effectiveness of these teams is increased because of total integration of school staff in the delivery of the programmes . . . Each school year has its own programme which builds on the previous year's teaching. In each year, there will be an agreed set vocabulary to be taught and developed. It is hoped that primary schools will be able to incorporate this new vocabulary into their literacy hours, and secondary schools will do the same into their English teaching programme. The pro-grammes aim to work in close conjunction with the schools' existing courses such as English and RE. (Building Bridges Pendle 2002, p. 4)

The team produced its own programme booklets for each year group. The booklets contained over 65 pages of materials includ-ing a copy of the mission statement, schemes of work for Citizen-ship Education and PSHE, an overview of the six sessions, a selection of teaching guidelines, some workshop activity sheets, several tables of statistics, three street maps, a series of newspaper cuttings and a feedback questionnaire. The booklets were intended as a reference source for teachers and were posted to the schools before the BBP team made its first visit. This gave the Citizenship teachers time to peruse the document and to consider whether they wanted to assist the team in the delivery of the programme.

In most of the schools, the team delivered the workshops without interference from teachers, though teachers and teaching assistants helped with the facilitation of activities.

The programme placed strong emphasis on how different communities could live together. The workshops were delivered in an interactive manner and contained four core modules; namely, *My World and Me, Conflict and Conflict Resolution, Social Behavioural Influences* and *Solutions*. Both the Year 6 and the Year 7 programmes contained icebreakers, stories, group exercises and role play activities. The aim of the Year 7 programme was to build on the knowledge gained in the previous year, although the repetition of certain themes allowed for the fact that some of the pupils had not (depending on which primary schools they had attended) received any former BBP input. In a small number of the workshops, the team included video footage, talks by local police officers and parental participation. In the *My World and Me* module, the sessions revolved around the issues of religious diversity, holy sites, personal identity, social harmony, cultural differences and demography. The *Conflict and Conflict Resolution* module included anger management, prejudice, discrimination, bullying and aversion strategies. The *Social Behavioural Influences* module addressed the issues of stereotyping, peer pressure, mob mentality, the role of the local community and the influence of agents of socialization. The final module (*Solutions*) aimed to promote a better understanding of reason, knowledge, empathy and interpersonal relations. It was in this module that the issues of religious cohesion and interfaith dialogue received the most attention.

The main strength of outreach programmes such as these is that they reflect local issues (immigration and asylum seeking were included in the BBP programme) which make young people aware of the importance of good community relations. In both the Year 6 and Year 7 programmes, the pupils were asked to reflect on the concepts of ethnicity, diversity, faith and identity as descriptors of the Pendle borough and to construct a list of landmarks (places of worship, restaurants, visitors' centres and the like) that could be used as indicators of religious and cultural diversity. In the first two workshops, the pupils were given street maps and tables of statistics indicating local settlement patterns and ethnic group profiles. These were accompanied by photographic images (presented in the form of a slideshow) of the local community.

The team's own evaluation confirmed that the majority of White pupils were surprised to learn that although two-thirds of the occupants of one ward were of Asian heritage, the total number of BME residents for the borough as a whole was only 14 per cent. The team used these demographic trends to challenge local and national misconceptions about the ethnic composition of the borough and to address the negative perceptions of Black and Asian communities.

The remaining workshops centred on the causes of ethnic and religious segregation and the undesirable consequences to which this segregation can give rise. According to the BBP co-ordinator, the most effective way of building on the issues raised in the first two sessions was to use scenario material that would help school pupils to understand the complexity of immigration and its impact on social relations. This strategy achieved positive results. Unlike the introductory sessions in which the pupils had been given textual information, the issues of immigration and settlement were addressed through a series of imaginary activities. In one activity, a Year 7 class was divided into small groups and asked to imagine that they were about to leave their homelands in search of a better life. The pupils were told that the country to which they would be migrating had initiated the invitation (mainly for the benefit its own economy) by offering employment contracts to migrant workers. Each group was required to complete a set of questions related to the scenario and to record their responses on a flip chart. During the exercise, the pupils were asked to consider how they would handle the emotional wrench of leaving their loved-ones (many of whom were elderly and living in poverty), what practical difficulties this would pose, which particular aspects of their culture they would want and could reasonably expect to retain once they had arrived in their new place of residence, what attempts they would make to establish positive relationships with members of the indigenous population, which civil activities, if any, they would want to avoid without causing offence, what steps they would take to ensure that they remained near to people who shared their cultural and religious heritage, what they would do to help their children adjust to a different way of life and a large number of other questions concerning economic migration.

The BBP team agreed that of all the workshops they delivered in the Pendle schools, this activity provided the most powerful means of challenging the deep-rooted misconceptions that had pervaded East Lancashire for the previous five decades and which many of the pupils had internalized. The team had chosen this activity in order to contextualize the history of immigration and to help the pupils understand the significance of the demographic data they had examined in the previous sessions. This strategy of linking macro social, economic and cultural events to the development of the local community offered an effective way of nurturing empathy and of improving the pupils' knowledge of historical and cultural processes. By the end of the scenario activity, the pupils were able to make sense of the settlement patterns that had occurred in the borough (which they had learnt were rooted in the textile industry) and the effects of these on community relations. The pupils recognized that for people of Asian heritage, particularly first generation members, the issues of immigration in the 1960s had revolved around economic stability. Despite having lived in Pendle all their lives, most of the White pupils had been unaware of the historical experiences of first generation BME residents and hence the reasons for the settlement of distinct ethnic and religious groups. Towards the end of the programme, issues such as housing tenancy, social and cultural relations, continued religious conviction and the expansion of local Pakistani and Bangladeshi businesses were seen in a different light.

By presenting the process of immigration and settlement as a historical narrative, the team had unravelled a complex story that had come as something of a revelation to a large number of pupils. This imaginary immigration exercise was, however, far more than a lesson in social history. The whole *raison d'etre* of BBP was to foster religious empathy and the workshop activities were intended to achieve this objective. The team recognized that didactic approaches to religious cohesion were unlikely, in an increasingly secular climate, to be successful. The failure of conventional religious knowledge to raise the profile of faith communities, and less still to help young people to respect religious diversity, was an issue to which several RE teachers in East Lancashire alluded. In one of the schools in which the questionnaire survey was conducted (detailed in Chapter 2), a sizable number of pupils were unable to distinguish between Hinduism and Islam despite having completed a unit on world religions. Moreover, a smaller but none the less significant number were unaware that Roman

Catholicism was a Christian denomination and that Protestantism extended beyond the Church of England. While one might be inclined to regard this lack of basic religious knowledge as an indictment on teachers, it is far more likely to be indicative of the widespread lack of interest in religious matters among large numbers of school pupils across the whole of the UK. The spiral model adopted by BBP implicitly acknowledges the religious apathy of young people and can, with appropriate planning, counter some of this resistance.[21] By challenging local stereotypes and misconceptions, the team was able to strip away the various layers of prejudice and help the pupils to empathize with people who had had a different experience to themselves.[22] In their attempt to promote a better understanding of immigration, this small group of outreach workers had, in fact, raised the profile of religious faith.

Summary

In this chapter, I have outlined a number of strategies adopted by schools and colleges for addressing religious diversity in the curriculum. My research in East Lancashire confirms that there is no blueprint for how this should be attempted and no guarantee that what works well in one establishment will work well in another. The profiles of students in a particular school or college may, however, be an indicator of the issues most worthy of inclusion. The bipolar demography of Burnley, Blackburn and Pendle manifests itself in ethnic, cultural and religious segregation and this highlights the need for educational initiatives that promote integration. This is no easy challenge in areas where cultural and national allegiances cause social divisions and where levels of cohesion vary within as well as between different groups. For this reason, some schools and colleges use cultural rather than religious activities (illustrated in all three sections of this chapter) in their quest to create a sense of belonging and to encourage students to recognize that *all* communities are of value in a modern pluralistic society. It seems that even schools and colleges with a religious constitution are aware of the complexities of religious belief and of the difficulties in approaching faith oriented issues in a doctrinal manner. To add to the complexity, faith schools represent some of the most culturally and ethnically diverse establishments in the UK.

My research reveals an incongruity between school composition and religious tolerance. The results of the questionnaire survey which my colleagues and I carried out in the first year of the investigation show that while one might expect to find a greater degree of racial and religious harmony in mixed schools, this is not necessarily the case. The views expressed by the pupils in the two mono-cultural schools could not have been more different, with pupils of Asian/Muslim heritage showing far higher levels of liberality and willingness to integrate than their White counterparts. The attitudes of the pupils in the mixed school lay somewhere in-between. In Burnley, it was the teachers working in schools that had the highest intake of White pupils who relayed the most disturbing anecdotes of ignorance and prejudice – attitudes that reflected an entrenched parochial perspective that had most likely been inherited from parents. On reflection, it is not surprising that these prejudices are voiced more openly in mono-cultural settings.

In the light of these findings, it is imperative that schools and colleges, wherever their location, pay renewed attention to how young people can be encouraged to respect cultural and religious diversity. The evidence suggests that the majority of pupils from Christian backgrounds are members of religious denominations by default (most often as a consequence of infant baptism), and that even second and subsequent generation Muslims are becoming increasingly reluctant to partake in institutional worship. This weakening of religious participation does not mean, however, that young people are no longer receptive to religious initiatives or that religious beliefs cease to play an important part in the lives of some pupils. In most of the schools and colleges in which my research was carried out, religious convictions among both staff and students ranged from very strong to non-existent, with much variation in-between. This makes the question of how Christian–Muslim unity can best be achieved in the education system all the more challenging. At present, the answer is to allow genuine advocates of religious cohesion (teachers, outreach workers and school chaplains) a stake in the agenda and to avoid activities that are likely to produce hostility. This is not to suggest that religious differences should not receive attention (paradoxically, some would argue that this is something faith partnerships ignore at their own peril), but that these need to be addressed in an appropriate manner. In the UK, schools in every sector are involved in a wide range of initiatives that aim to avert the fear of difference, broaden cultural horizons and tackle social segregation. Religious cohesion, whatever form this might take, can make a worthy contribution to these important social and political objectives.

Notes

1 The most progressive of these initiatives were advanced by local authorities such as Brent and the ILEA.

2 This was part of the rationale for the introduction of Citizenship Education by the Blair government in 2002.

3 At present, there are several world faiths components on most approved RE syllabuses for secondary education.

4 By cross-school/college policies, I mean where *all* teaching staff are expected to contribute to the delivery of multifaith/multicultural education.

5 Despite widespread publicity and several weeks notice, the event was poorly attended with only half the teachers previously interviewed present. None the less, the BBB officers made subsequent contact with all the schools to offer outreach support for the remainder of the year.

6 The teachers most aware of this were employed in mono-cultural schools.

7 AS and A Level Religious Studies syllabuses are, as one would expect, more demanding than GCSE.

8 In the light of this confusion, the time may have come to replace subject titles such as *Religious Education* and *Religious Studies* with something like *Cultural Studies* – a multidisciplinary curriculum area that often features in Higher Education prospectuses and which could include the study of religion in its various forms.

9 Seemingly, this debate led to a political discussion about the concept of religious freedom – an issue that had caused a political furore in France some 18 months or so earlier with the banning of headscarves in state schools.

10 Hence, the justification for arranged marriages in the eyes of some (though by no means all) Muslim students.

11 Unlike academic programmes, NVQs are intended to enhance the student's ability to acquire competences for specific types of employment.

12 The workshop materials included multiple-choice questionnaire on faith and ethnicity, profiles of well-known religious leaders, worksheets on racial and religious prejudice, scenario-based tasks on racism and intolerance and a range of other activities concerning ethics and religious rights.

13 See www.qca.org.uk/7907.html for schemes of work for Citizenship Education. Key Stage 3 Units 3, 4, 11 and 13 and Key Stage 4 Units 1 and 3 all lend themselves to faith oriented discussions that could be tailored to reflect the religious and ethnic composition of a given locality.

14 It should be borne in mind that the subject was, at this time, relatively new and that almost all the staff responsible for its delivery in Burnley were teachers of other subjects.

15 For an analysis of some of the more recent strategies adopted by Roman Catholic schools in the formation of Citizenship Education, see O'Keeffe and Zipfel (2007).

16 One possible solution to this problem would be to employ subject specialists with designated responsibility for delivery. In the present climate, this could be achieved by allowing Social Science graduates (most of whom are employed in the post-16 sector) to enter secondary education where their knowledge and expertise of citizenship issues would be of value.

17 Quoted from a booklet produced by the Head of Citizenship.

18 The Youth Development Officer was a former high school teacher and Head of Religious Studies.

19 This was almost half of the primary and secondary schools in the Pendle borough.

20 The most significant of which had been the settlement of BME communities within the past four decades.

21 The spiral model is an approach that attempts to build on knowledge previously attained.

22 In January 2005, the team leader together with the Director of Evaluation Studies at the University of Huddersfield designed a pupil feedback questionnaire which they used to establish the extent to which the programme had achieved its objectives. The results of the questionnaire were encouraging. A comparison of the baseline and post-intervention scores revealed a marked improvement in attitude in 43.1 per cent of the respondents. The most significant changes were found in pupils who had attended more than half the sessions

and who had entered the programme with the poorest baseline scores (Kazi and Eades, 2005). Although there have been few official studies on the effectiveness of outreach provision in British schools and colleges, these results suggest that faith partnerships can make a valuable contribution to the curriculum. In this sense, the BBP approach echoes the contributory model.

4. The Spirit of the North: an interfaith initiative for young adults

At the Global Summit in June 1996, a 10-year-old boy created an origami logo from a multi-coloured sheet of paper. The boy took the paper, cut out a circle, and made several folds to produce a star-shaped design in which the colours blended together. On completion of his design, the boy announced:

> Once, the religions were far apart. These different coloured pieces are like all different religions. Slowly, the religions get closer to understanding each other. And when they understand and make peace with each other, there will be something no one expected – a star! (United Religions Initiative, 2001)

Unintentionally, this young boy had provided the constitutional philosophy for an organization that would become known as *The United Religions Initiative* (URI) – an international faith partnership. The first URI gathering in the UK was held at a three day conference at St George's House, Windsor, in 1998, where consultations were held between politicians and religious representatives. The purpose of the consultations was to discuss religious unity. After a period of networking and the completion of several pilot projects, the trustees produced a 5-year business plan. The formal launch of the organization was held at the Greenwich Dome in August 2000 where 400 people from different faith communities gathered to witness the signing of the URI charter. The organization was granted UK registered charity status in 2001 and has since received a substantial amount of funding for the facilitation of interfaith initiatives.[1]

The URI is committed to the promotion of religious cohesion at global, regional and local levels. Its charter states:

> Working on all continents and across continents, people from different religions, spiritual expressions and indigenous traditions are creating unprecedented levels of enduring global co-operation. Today, at its birth, people's hopes are rising with visions of a better world. It is a world where the values and teachings of the great wisdom traditions guide people's service, where people respect one another's beliefs, and where the resourcefulness and passion of ordinary people working together bring healing and a more hopeful future to the Earth community. The URI, in time, aspires to have the visibility of the United Nations.
>
> Since June 1996, thousands of people have shared their visions and worked together to create the URI. It is a new kind of organization for global good, rooted in shared spiritual values. People from many different cultures and perspectives have worked to create an organization that is inclusive, non-hierarchical and de-centralised; one that enhances co-operation autonomy and individual opportunity. This co-creative work offered by people of many cultures has produced a unique organization composed of self-organising groups which operate locally and are connected globally. (United Religions Initiative, 2001)

Like all faith partnerships, the URI encourages people from different religious backgrounds to share their existential perspectives and to identify common humanitarian values. In its attempt to achieve this, the organization emphasizes spirituality rather than religiosity – an approach that attracts followers of New Age movements as well as members of monotheistic and polytheistic world faiths. The initiatives launched by the URI are of three principal kinds: (1) the creation of sacred spaces, (2) cross-generational dialogue and (3) projects for young people. The directors endorse the view that every faith community is able to contribute something of value to humanity and to the spiritual development of other religious groups.

The sharing of sacred space is something many religious organizations advocate. Buildings and holy grounds symbolizing peace, hope, wonder, mystery and fellowship bring large numbers of people together in community and celebration. Between 2001 and 2007, the URI established a number of these spaces. In 2005, the directors were offered 12 sq. m of ground in a building in Cheetham Hill, Manchester, for interfaith seminars and retreats. Leaders of Sikh, Jewish, Christian and Muslim communities began to explore different ways of using sacred spaces to attract members of other religious faiths. On a wider scale, the organization entered into a series of consultations with the Forestry Commission in the hope of creating some additional sites in the north of England. By 2006, three areas each of 50 ha were identified as potential holy grounds to be shared by around 100 faith communities.[2]

In addition to encouraging faith communities to share scared spaces, the URI is also renowned for organizing cross-generational workshops. The slogan *Spiritual Elders Meet Emerging Visionaries* is used to encourage dialogue between people of different age groups. The events take place in different areas of the UK and take the form of a 40 minute exchange between two strangers. The process begins with the elder encouraging the younger to share his or her spiritual perspectives. The exchange takes place in a quiet setting and is bound by a pledge of confidentiality between the two parties. The URI propounds the view that this is not an opportunity to proselytize or to unburden wrongdoing, but a chance for two individuals to share their spiritual stories. Each party is free to mention key individuals – religious writers, gurus, faith leaders and the like – who have been sources of inspiration and/or have offered spiritual guidance during a difficult period. Narratives of doubt, fear, hope and expectation may be included in the exchange. At the end of the activity, the couples agree to host a similar event in another location. By the winter of 2005, the organization had hosted cross-generational seminars in Newcastle, Birmingham, Nottingham, Manchester, London, Oxford and Cambridge for more than 100 participants.

The URI initiative that is of most relevance to this book is a project known as *The Spirit of the North* – an initiative for adults between the ages of 16 and 30 years. The aim of the project is to encourage young people from different religious backgrounds to take part in a series of interactive workshops. At the end of the project, the participants are asked to present their results (usually in the form of a photographic exhibition) to local stakeholders.[3] There are no prescribed rules about how the project is to be organized or what should be produced at the end. The trustees endorse the view that interfaith workshops are an effective way of uniting young people and of raising the profile of faith communities at local level. Since the projects are funded on limited resources, the participants are required to complete their activities (including their presentation) within a 2–3 month period. The advantages of this short time-scale are not just financial. Short-term projects are more likely to sustain motivation if participants are aware that their outcomes must be achieved by a certain date, thus increasing the likelihood of completion. By the end of 2005, the URI had facilitated 18 projects in the north of England.

The Spirit of Blackburn

The Spirit of the North project took place in Blackburn in the spring of 2005. Like Burnley, Blackburn had a majority Christian population, a relatively high number of Asian/Muslim residents and a smaller number of Hindus, Buddhists, Sikhs and Jews. This religious diversity made Blackburn a prime location for the project, the aims of which were:

1. to support the involvement of young adults in citizenship, entrepreneurial work, lateral thinking and leadership;
2. to encourage a change in attitude within the entire community (particularly among young adults) to the concept of diversity so that it is seen as a blessing not a threat;
3. to encourage and support the development of the Blackburn with Darwen Interfaith Council to ensure a lasting legacy and a more integrated local context; and,
4. to build support and financial commitment to the project in order to provide a solid foundation on which to tour the Spirit of the North exhibition in other northern towns and cities.
   (Centre for Local Economic Strategies (CLES) 2005, p. 23)

Despite an aggressive marketing campaign, the URI failed to recruit a sufficient number of young people from a mix of faith backgrounds to make the project viable in the Blackburn area. As a contingency strategy, the Chief Executive advertised to appoint a project worker for a 3-month period. The job description identified facilitation skills, personal understanding of interfaith work, experience of working with young people and photographic knowledge as essential criteria and welcomed applications from the statutory and voluntary sectors. The process of short-listing proved more difficult than expected, but the post was offered on a part-time basis to a Photography lecturer at Blackburn College of Further Education who agreed to lead the project as part of his lecturing duties.

The project would take the form of a photographic assignment based on the theme of spirituality and on the contribution of people of faith to the social and economic landscape of the town. The assignment would incorporate the concepts of cohesion, integration and spirituality and the material would be presented in the form of a public exhibition. If all went to plan, the assignment would widen the students' knowledge of spirituality and bring them into contact with different religious communities. The Chief Executive appealed for recruits through the Town Hall, the library, civic centres, local churches and the Lancashire Council of Mosques.

Disappointingly, the recruits were far from representative of the Blackburn borough. In the end, 16 students from the college itself, all of whom were aged between 16 and 19 years, were assigned the project as part of their programme of study. These were White students from Christian, agnostic and atheistic backgrounds. The absence of Asian/Muslim recruits was by far the most serious shortcoming given that, like Burnley, Islam represented the town's second largest faith community. There is widespread agreement in the UK that events such as 9/11, the war in Iraq, the London bombings and the northern disturbances call for a much deeper understanding of the beliefs of British Muslims and the Spirit of the North project would have provided an ideal opportunity for believers and non-believers alike to share their religious views. Despite the absence of Muslim participants, the project went ahead.

The project comprised a series of workshops focusing on the production of visual images. Throughout the project, the students were asked to take a large number of photographs of people in different religious settings. The photographs showed people praying, meditating, lighting candles, singing hymns, reading sacred texts and a whole host of other activities. The students were than asked to take photographs of the same devotees in work-based settings in order to promote an understanding of the contribution that people of faith made to the local community. This combination of sacred and secular images would demonstrate the interplay between religious and secular life. Throughout the course of the next 8 weeks, the students developed several hundred photographs of Christians, Muslims, Jews, Hindus, Sikhs, Buddhists, Wiccans and Baha'is in a wide range of religious and secular contexts. At the end of the project, a total of 30 photographs were selected and mounted on display boards in preparation for the exhibition. The photographs were then enlarged and labelled with a description of the devotee and the name of the photographer.

Like many other voluntary initiatives, the project contained a number of strengths and weaknesses. The URI directors commissioned a private company known as the Centre for Local Economic Strategies (CLES) to carry out an independent evaluation. The CLES team produced a lengthy document commenting on the extent to which the project had met its objectives. While the report commended the quality of the exhibition, several critical points were raised about the operation of the assignment. One of the main criticisms was that the project had been undertaken during the summer examination revision period and that no attempt had been made to track the number of hours spent by each participant. Subsequent interviews with the participants led the CLES team to conclude that some of the students had failed to make anything other than a tenuous contribution to the exhibition product.[4]

Despite the imbalance in religious and ethnic group profiles and inequities in workload, the evaluation report commended the participants for raising the profile of faith in Blackburn and for producing an innovative display. The exhibition was launched at the Town Hall in the summer of 2005 and attended by the Mayor and Mayoress of the local council. The event attracted around 60 people with representation from the town's different faith communities. An unusually large number of young people attended the event, among whom were the participants and their friends and relatives. The event included speeches by the Mayor and various members of the Interfaith Council who spoke about the importance of linking faith-based projects to other community initiatives. The highlight of the event was the input from the participants themselves who spoke about the opportunity that the assignment had given them to engage with people from different religious groups and how this had aided their understanding of cultural and religious diversity.

Though it is difficult to measure the success of a largely experiential initiative such as this, it was clear from the evaluation feedback and from the exhibition itself that most of the project outcomes had been met. The participants claimed that the project had boosted their self-confidence and that they had overcome their anxieties about meeting members of different religious groups (CLES, 2005, pp. 23–24). This suggests a positive shift in attitude among the participants and a willingness to confront previously held prejudices and preconceptions. If the comments of these participants are to be taken at face value, the contribution of the project to local community relations and to the involvement of young people in activities that have a religious dimension is encouraging.

The most difficult outcomes for the CLES team to assess were those concerning the longer term impact of the project and the extent to which its successes could benefit other towns and cities. The team concluded that it was difficult for external agencies to support the development of the Interfaith Council since this had not long been established. Moreover, organizations such as the URI were not sufficiently funded to provide the kind of support necessary for young people to achieve their full potential. Until such time that the Interfaith Council was able to increase its membership and attract more funding, its ability to support projects such as the Spirit of Blackburn was, according to the CLES report, limited. Be this as it may, the Chief Executive of the URI managed to launch the exhibition to a large group of stakeholders at St Ethelburga's Peace Centre in London.[5]

From the point of view of this book, the main strength of the Spirit of Blackburn project was its success in raising religious awareness among a group of young people for whom religious beliefs were largely non-existent. This validates the view that religious cohesion activities that work best in secular environments are those that allow participants to create their own agenda and take ownership of the content. By helping young people to channel their secular interests (in this case, photography) into a faith-oriented initiative, an appreciation of and respect for religious beliefs was achieved. As far as this project was concerned, an issue that has the potential to unite or divide large numbers of people – religious conviction – was presented to a group of students as part of their programme of study. As serendipity would have it, the failure of Blackburn to attract religious devotees made for a useful comparison with Burnley, where the approach to the same initiative could not have been more different. In a secular society, however, the Blackburn project represents one of the most realistic ways of helping young people to appreciate religious diversity.

The Spirit of Burnley

When the Spirit of Blackburn project was drawing to a close, the URI Chief Executive began to make some tenuous contact with faith partnerships in other local towns. His aim was to introduce the initiative to neighbouring localities in the hope that it would help challenge religious prejudice and encourage integration. Ambitious though these objectives were, if the project could be delivered successfully and the results disseminated to wide-enough audiences, the URI would have contributed something of value to the community cohesion effort.

The Spirit of the North arrived in Burnley only a few weeks after the Blackburn participants had presented their exhibition. The prospect of launching the project in a neighbouring town was an opportunity for the URI team to reflect on the experience of Blackburn and to consider what, if anything, could be done differently. Though the Blackburn project achieved many positive outcomes, its failure to recruit Muslim participants was by far its greatest weakness. There were two reasons why this should not be repeated in Burnley. First, it had not been forgotten that it was Asian and White youths who were the main protagonists of the 2001 disturbances – an event that did nothing to alleviate the segregation that had characterized the town for several decades. While there was no knowing the depth of religious faith among the dissidents themselves, any cohesion initiative that could recruit a cross-section of young people from different ethnic and religious backgrounds could only improve social relations. The second point is related indirectly to the first. Like Blackburn, Burnley was home to a large number of Muslim residents, most of whom were of Pakistani heritage. Since Muslims represented the second largest faith in the borough, the project could, with sufficient interest from both communities, help to create a stronger sense of cohesion.

Recruitment for the Spirit of Burnley began with a chance meeting between the Chief Executive of the URI and a local youth and community officer – a well-known and hugely respected figure in the borough who was already involved in several other local initiatives for young people. This fortuitous alliance would prove to be one of the biggest contributors to the project's success. The youth officer (also a member of BBB) informed her colleagues of the prospect of launching the project in Burnley and with the support of a small number of volunteers, began a recruitment campaign. In the next few weeks, she distributed URI leaflets to community centres, places of worship, voluntary agencies, the local library, the college of Further Education, the Youth Service and several other organizations that she felt might attract prospective recruits. After several weeks of marketing, two introductory meetings were held at one of the town's youth and community centres. The meetings attracted around 20 young people from Christian and Muslim backgrounds.

Despite some initial reservations on the part of the Chief Executive, the Burnley recruits decided that their project would take the form of a residential retreat and that they would prepare their exhibition in the post-residential period. The participants were unanimous in the view that a neutral venue would provide an appropriate environment in which they could eat, chat, exchange humour and take part in a number of activities that would enable them to share their faith. They agreed that a weekend conference in an attractive residential setting would allow them to engage with each other more fully than would be possible in a community centre or a place of worship. The Chief Executive suggested that Whalley Abbey – a fourteenth century monastery situated in the heart of the Ribble Valley some 10 or so miles from Burnley – would be an ideal venue. The Abbey was used for business conferences and residential retreats and boasted high class accommodation. The rural location of the venue offered a tranquil environment in which the participants would feel far enough from home to appreciate the full benefits of a retreat. Though they all possessed mobile phones, the participants agreed that these would be used only for incoming calls and emergencies. The Chief Executive volunteered to make some provisional enquiries about the availability of the venue and offered to subsidize the event from the URI budget.

By the end of their second meeting, the participants identified two main objectives of the project. These were:

1. to create a better understanding of each other's faith perspectives; and
2. to raise awareness of the contribution of faith to the local community.

The next 2 months were used to plan the conference programme and to identify the essential tasks. A final cohort of 16 young people (9 Muslims and 7 Christians) registered for the retreat and a weekend booking was made at the venue.[6]Although the project organizers were disappointed that they had been unable to attract people from faith communities other than Muslim and Christian, they were at least satisfied that the group reflected the main religious composition (and bipolar nature) of the town.

In addition to the differences in religious membership, there were wide variations in age. The youngest and eldest participants appeared at opposite ends of the age continuum with a fairly even distribution in-between. Eight of the participants were aged between 18 and 21 years, six between the ages of 22 and 25 years and the remaining two were in the 26–30 age group. The occupational groups were less representative with 9 of the 16 participants employed as youth workers and the remaining seven studying full-time in further or higher education. Despite the limited occupational and religious profiles, the age and gender variations ensured that this was a more representative group than might otherwise have been the case.

Of the 16 participants, 6 were elected as facilitators (3 from each faith community) to work with the directors in preparing a programme of interfaith activities. The facilitators were mindful of the diversity of beliefs within as well as between the two groups (particularly between the Christian participants who were members of different denominations) and of differences in the nature and extent of religious worship. The facilitators agreed that the conference should be of a non-proselytizing nature and that every effort should be made to give equal representation to the two faith traditions. It was decided that each facilitator would lead a different activity and collate the feedback once the tasks had been completed. Although there was no official code of practice, some general principles were established concerning the rights of individuals to withdraw from any activities in which they did not wish to partake. The group decided that no alcohol would be consumed during the workshop periods and that the residential activities would not coincide with prayer times. As a mark of respect to the Muslim participants, the facilitators made a request to the venue proprietors that all food would meet halal requirements and that a vegetarian option would be available. Within the next few weeks, a programme of icebreakers, interfaith activities and exhibition workshops had been prepared by the facilitators.

THE RESIDENTIAL

On the Friday evening of the residential, the 16 participants congregated at Whalley Abbey. They were accompanied by two Anglican priests (one of whom was the URI Chief Executive), two project directors and the BBB co-ordinator. Of these five extra participants, all but the Chief Executive were active BBB members and most had had experience of working with teenagers and young adults.

The participants arrived at the venue at around 5.30 pm and were shown to their rooms by the Abbey staff. The Abbey was owned by the Anglican Diocese of Blackburn and comprised several impressive buildings. The ruins of the old monastery were open to the general public and surrounded by well-tended gardens and walkways. On the Abbey site was a visitors' centre, a coffee shop, a picnic area and a nature trail. The walls of the conference rooms were decorated with wooden panels and the ceilings were supported by original beams. In the basement was a chapel, a library, a kitchen and a dining room. The Abbey provided an ideal venue for the retreat.

INTRODUCTION AND ICEBREAKERS

The programme for the Friday evening included dinner followed by a series of icebreakers. The icebreaker session was introduced by the Chief Executive and facilitated by Salma, a Muslim participant who worked as a Community Development Officer in the voluntary sector. The Chief Executive began by asking the question: Why are we here? He gave a short address on 'the dangers of secularism' in which he talked about the commodification of human beings and the excesses of material wealth. He warned of the consequences of financial greed and power and expressed his belief that God was in danger of being excluded from the public and the private spheres of life. At the end of his address, he appealed to the participants to use the weekend to unite in faith and to demonstrate this unity to the people of Burnley. At this point, he asked Salma to introduce the icebreakers.

The first icebreaker was entitled *Things about me*. In this session, each participant was asked to make four very brief and completely random statements about themselves to the rest of the group. These could be descriptions of their families, favourite holiday destinations, tastes in music, food preferences, hobbies, likes and dislikes, best achievements, worst disasters or whatever other issues the participants chose to mention. Although the four random details offered by each participant made for 25 minutes of humour, the session had two serious objectives. First, it allowed the participants to learn more about each other in a relaxed atmosphere; and second, it gave them an opportunity to share their biographies with people from different ethnic and religious groups. Although only a handful of the participants made reference to their religious beliefs in their statements, the fact that they volunteered personal information enabled their peers to recognize that religious conviction was only one aspect of their identity and that there was a vast range of parallel issues – educational achievements, sporting and leisure activities, travel, media interests and many others – that united the group. In this respect, the icebreaker helped to contextualize religious faith through an activity that would not normally have taken place.

The second icebreaker involved the use of a modern electronic gadget that has come to be regarded as an essential item by millions of people worldwide – the mobile phone. Although the participants had agreed to keep their mobile phones switched off during conference activities, Salma was aware that everyone in the group owned one and decided to prepare an activity that would involve its usage. In this icebreaker, each participant was asked to activate his/her phone and to justify to the group his/her choice of ring tone. On the surface, this seemed a rather frivolous exercise, but as soon as the activity started, it was clear that behind many of these few bars of music was a personal story. Among the ring tones were religious melodies, rock music and sports themes. The ring tones revealed a surprisingly large amount of information about the participants.

The title of Salma's third icebreaker was *Your name*. In this activity, the participants were asked to introduce their forenames and to explain why their names had been chosen by their parents. Details included the origin and meaning of the name, its place in the participant's family history and its usage among friends and relatives. As the activity began to unfold, it was clear that the participants knew the meaning of their names and why their parents had chosen it for them. Behind many of the participants' names was a piece of family history and some of the names were associated with a place or a philosophical concept.[7] Almost half of the Christian participants had been named after a saint, a biblical character or a well-known public figure. Three people claimed that their names had been a source of ridicule during their school years and one participant admitted to changing her name when she was younger because she had disliked it so much. These stories produced much laughter and revealed some interesting snippets of information about the recruits.

The final icebreaker involved an activity which Salma called *Worship*. Unlike the previous three icebreakers, this was a group activity in which the participants were asked to divide into subgroups and to elect a rapporteur. The four groups were given the task of designing a poster depicting the theme of worship, the purpose of which was to allow the two faith communities to explore similarities and differences between each other's religious traditions. After half an hour of intense group interaction, four large illustrations were produced by the participants and presented to the rest of the group. The first group (a group of male Muslims) prepared their design in green which they had chosen because it was the colour of Islam. Their display contained illustrations of seeds and trees which were used to depict growth and which the participants explained was a metaphor for worship. The second group (the female Muslims) presented a rather busier display containing illustrations of light (representing Allah), a mosque, some prayer beads and a globe. For this group, these images represented the universality of worship. The third group (the male Christians) prepared a poster containing illustrations of water (depicting the cleansing power of worship), a map (representing universality), several bars of music and a loaf of bread. Like their Muslim counterparts, this group used symbols from their own religious tradition. The final group (the female Christians) created a design depicting fire (a symbol of the Holy Spirit), a crucifix and a Bible.

The *Worship* activity achieved several outcomes, the most important of which was that it enabled the participants to explore common ground. Since no one member of any group knew all the other participants, the task encouraged *intra*-faith as well as an interfaith dialogue. It was the Christian (sub)-groups to which this applied most, since these participants differed most in their religious beliefs and practices. Notwithstanding these intra-faith differences, the exercise unearthed several commonalities. The theme of worship allowed the participants the opportunity to express their beliefs and to acknowledge that they all paid homage to an omnipotent deity. They also recognized that religious symbols – buildings, physical objects, music, clothing, sacred texts and so forth – were important to both traditions and that the styles of worship were universal.

It became apparent during this last icebreaker that almost any religious concept – sin, salvation, suffering, morality, charity, integrity, penitence, grace or any other – could have been used to initiate dialogue between the two groups. A more generous allocation of time, or indeed an activity that extended the boundaries of an icebreaking session, would have allowed the participants the chance to discuss specific aspects of worship (fasting, pilgrimages, festivals and dedication rituals, for example), and perhaps even to witness some of these in practice. The icebreakers did, however, help to create an atmosphere of trust on which friendships could be built.

CROSSING THE RELIGIOUS DIVIDE

The Saturday itinerary included three workshops, two of which were held in the morning and one in the afternoon. The main purpose of the day was to provide an opportunity for the participants to work together on a series of interfaith activities. Each workshop was scheduled to last for an hour and a half, the last 15 minutes of which were allocated to feedback. Like the final icebreaker of the previous evening, two of the workshops comprised group tasks, but in these activities, the participants worked with members of a different faith community. The aim of these activities was to build on the friendships that had started to be formed. Each session began with a scriptural/koranic reading or a short piece of music.

The first workshop was introduced as the *Faith and Culture Share* and was the only Saturday activity that did not involve group interaction. The seeds for this session had been sown some weeks earlier when, on receiving copies of the programme, the participants had been asked to bring along to the conference a cultural or religious artefact such as a picture, a poem, a sacred text, an item of clothing or a piece of jewellery. The participants were informed that at some point during the conference, they would each be asked to introduce their object and to talk about its significance. The facilitators had made a conscious decision to allow the participants to present a religious *or* a cultural object in order to accommodate those whose religious beliefs were not very clearly defined. Whatever their choice of item, it was hoped that the participants would share a small part of their life narrative (building on the objectives of the first two icebreakers) before attempting the group tasks.

Within an hour or so, each participant (including the directors) had introduced his or her object and spoken about its personal value. Among the objects were prayer books, meditation aids, photographs, icons, philosophical poems, cultural and/or religious magazines, items of clothing (including headscarves and small caps worn by Muslims), prayer mats, rosary beads, copies of sacred texts, diaries, crucifixes and a large number of inspirational writings. Most of these objects were of sentimental value (the most common of which were gifts from friends and relatives) and almost three quarters were items of memorabilia. In contrast with the icebreakers, the culture share was a sedate activity which provided insights into the personalities and identities of the participants. At the end of the session, the objects were placed on a large coffee table and left for people to peruse at their own leisure. A photograph of the items was then taken by one of the facilitators in preparation for the exhibition.

The Faith and Culture Share aroused considerable interest and helped lay the foundation for the remaining activities of the day. The participants who had brought along textual materials such as biblical passages or philosophies talked of how they had been affected by what they had read and how the words had helped them to cope with a particular situation or event. A small number of participants associated a poem or a koranic verse with the death of a loved-one or with an important life decision. At no time did any of the participants attempt to use their belongings to proselytize or to advance a personal cause. The evaluation questionnaires distributed and completed at the end of the event revealed that half of the participants identified the culture share as the most insightful activity of the weekend. This suggests that cross-faith/cultural events that allow individuals the freedom to express themselves in informal settings are an effective way of challenging prejudices and averting segregation. The success of this activity owed much to the fact that the participants chose their own objects and were never, at any time, asked to offer anything other than a brief testimony.

The second workshop was entitled *The Contribution of Faith to our Lives*. In this session, the participants were divided into four mixed faith groups and asked to brainstorm some of the ways in which their religious beliefs impacted on their daily thoughts and actions. The participants were asked to reflect on the most rewarding aspects of their faith as well as the challenges it presented. The aim of the activity was to provide an opportunity for the participants to share their religious experiences and to identify which of these experiences they had in common. At the end of the activity, the participants presented a précis of their discussion on a flip chart.

The participants agreed that the biggest part of their daily lives was spent either at home or at work and there were some interesting similarities and differences between the four groups. The participants all maintained that their religious beliefs gave them a feeling of well-being and that this was something they would not want to lose. Several of the participants claimed that their faith had been strengthened by events that brought them close to their relatives, the most common of which were family bereavements and the termination of relationships. The Muslim participants claimed that it was the uniformity of their beliefs and the sense of belonging to a worldwide religious community (referred to in Islam as the *umma*) that helped them to deal with the most difficult life challenges. Like some of the Christian participants, however, they conceded that there had been times in their lives when they had found it difficult to remain steadfast in their faith and that they had always been mindful of the tension between the austerity of Islam and the secularity of the West. Participants from both faith communities agreed that the most challenging aspects of being a Muslim or a Christian included the demand for sexual purity, the appeal for regular prayer and, most difficult of all, the obligation to show kindness to their adversaries.

Above and beyond the peace and solidarity which the two groups claimed their religious beliefs provided, there were other important similarities that the participants identified in this activity. As the dialogue continued, it became apparent that both faith communities placed a strong emphasis on tolerance, respect, charity, patience, symbolic cleanliness, forgiveness and most important of all, loving one's neighbour. Although the participants were mindful of their doctrinal differences, there was an acknowledgement that Christianity and Islam had evolved from the same Abrahamic tradition and that God's love for humankind offered hope for the future. The participants also agreed that the Islamic concept of *jihad* (striving in the path of Allah) and the Christian principle of 'walking with Jesus' had profound similarities and that religious diversity should not prevent people from different faith communities from supporting each other. This group task had, fortuitously or otherwise, enabled the participants to identify common themes from their different religious traditions.

The aim of the third workshop was to place the issues raised in the previous activity in a broader context. This activity was called *The Impact of Faith on the Local Community* – an activity in which the participants were asked to provide examples of how their religious beliefs formed the basis of community action. A lengthy discussion followed of the difficulties young people faced in living out their faith in an ephemeral world of materialism, hedonism and immediate gratification. In three of the four groups, the Muslim participants talked of how the five pillars of Islam (particularly fasting during Ramadan and the obligation to pray five times a day) required vigilance and self-discipline, especially in secular environments. There followed a heated discussion about the extent to which Islam needed to adapt to secular modernity – a discussion which again demonstrates the value of dialogue within as well as between religious groups.[8]

The participants went on to discuss the different ways in which they felt their faith could be demonstrated in the local community. One of the most interesting examples was that of dress codes. All but one of the female Muslim participants, for example, wore a headscarf during the conference, and most said they wore it at all times in public. One young woman explained that she felt incompletely dressed without her hijab and that she had difficulty going about her daily business if it was not fastened around her head properly. The koranic appeal for modest dress presented these Muslim women with an opportunity to talk about the symbolic significance of their clothing and how it helped them to affirm their identity. Though, unlike their Muslim counterparts, the young Christian women did not wear head coverings, they agreed that modest dress was an important religious requisite that was substantiated in biblical texts.

In addition to their respective Christian and Islamic beliefs, the participants all confirmed their respect for secular law. The group presentations made reference, implicitly or explicitly, to the importance of acting with honesty and integrity in public places. As far as employment was concerned, the participants agreed that the making of money through dishonest means (an issue that violates the principles both of Islam and Christianity) was one of the worst examples a person of faith could set to others. The participants also felt that tackling anti-social behaviour within their own neighbourhoods was part and parcel of their spiritual mission and that religious leaders needed to work together to this end. Some of the participants expressed concern about the absence of role-models in faith communities and felt that if younger people could make a more conscious effort to understand each other's religious traditions, Burnley would be a better place. One of the project facilitators suggested that it might be possible at the end of the exhibition for the participants to establish an interfaith consortium with a view to addressing some of these issues.

Perhaps the most important issue to emerge from this third workshop, however, was that of how faith was represented in public services. All four groups approached this issue in different ways and made a number of suggestions about how things could improve. The first group was keen to raise the profile of faith throughout the voluntary sector. The participants felt that with the formation of appropriate structures, young people would be able to promote community cohesion through faith-based initiatives. Though the participants agreed that this would require joined up thinking, they were united in the view that Burnley already had a large number of youth projects (many of which had been implemented since the 2001 disturbances and had attracted a large amount of funding) to which faith communities could make a significant contribution. While the participants recognized that BBB had made an effort to do this, they were concerned that this was a partnership of mainly older people (some of whom were ordained ministers) and that faith representation was limited.

The second group focused much more on the role of religious institutions at local level. This group felt that churches and mosques were becoming increasingly marginalized and debated whether this was a symptom or a cause of secularization. There was general agreement among the participants that religious institutions were failing to attract young people, partly because society had been hijacked by a largely secular media, but also because religious leaders were out of touch with their own communities. There were, however, some subtle differences in the way these concerns were voiced. Arif and Rubina (the two Muslim participants) made the point that mosques could do more to include women in religious activities and worship. They felt that although women were free to enter mosques, few were comfortable in doing so. Rubina expressed the view that Muslim women, young and old, tended to worship at home because of their busy domestic roles and because of their primary responsibility for child care. She argued that this was particularly inhibiting for older Muslim women who had not been educated in British schools and who often felt excluded from public life. Rubina believed that one way of redressing this would be to introduce interfaith activities in places of worship; initially in mosques where non-English speaking women could attend with their daughters and granddaughters with whom they would not feel intimidated.

Arif and Rubina went on to raise what they saw as the central issue in this debate; namely, the inability of Muslim leaders to engage with people of younger generations. Both expressed concern over the way in which Islamic beliefs were imparted by imams and other religious leaders. Arif's recollection of what he described as his 'childhood indoctrination' in which he was required to learn koranic texts by rote (and in Arabic) had made him critical of traditional religious leadership which he felt hindered younger British Muslims. The two Christian participants, Deborah and Martin, concurred with this in respect of their own religious communities. Though they belonged to different denominations (the Baptist and the Methodist Church, respectively), Deborah and Martin agreed that a large number of Christian churches were failing not only to attract worshippers, but to retain the very few young people who still attended. Deborah explained that while the minister of her own church was approachable; he, like many other Christian ministers, placed great emphasis on family values and biblical edicts. Although Deborah still attended church, her attendance had become rather sporadic and she had stopped reading her bible on a daily basis. Moreover, Deborah's parents had been separated for some years and her recollection of their constant squabbling caused her to question her minister's conservative approach. Deborah continued to attend church because she claimed she needed God and enjoyed being part of a Christian community, but at the same time, she doubted whether conservative Christianity would continue to attract young people like herself who had grown up in a town that seemed to offer few prospects.

Like Deborah, Martin felt that religious leaders, nationally and locally, were failing to reach 'problem families' and that this was leading to the demise of Christianity. Although Martin lived in a more affluent suburb of Burnley than Deborah and had, in fact, graduated from University the previous year, he was also aware of the economic deprivation that bedevilled the inner wards of the borough and agreed that churches were not seen as the most inviting of places among those who had experienced the worst effects of social exclusion. Martin questioned whether Christian ministers were doing as much as they could to reach disaffected young people and lone-parent families and felt that Muslim leaders also needed to respond to family diversity if they were to have any hope of transcending cultural and religious boundaries.

The discussion in the third group revolved much more around the role of faith communities in health and education. These participants believed that although imams and Christian leaders made an important contribution to local hospitals, there were opportunities for lay people to offer support to patients and relatives. One participant felt that the aging population had resulted in a widening ratio of religious leaders to hospital patients (exacerbated by the fact that Christianity was attracting fewer people than ever before into religious ministry) and that priests and vicars were already overburdened with pastoral responsibilities. The group felt that although the pressure on the voluntary sector was substantial, religious volunteers could, with sufficient funding, provide additional pastoral support and that this would help to improve faith and ethnic relations across local authorities. The group also expressed the need for faith provision to be extended to the residential care sector in the hope that this would unite the young and the elderly, but were wary of the dangers of transferring the responsibility for this provision away from health trusts and other care providers.

Education was the other area of the public sector to which this group felt faith communities could make a contribution. The participants believed that as far as the long term future was concerned, it was school children who needed to be made aware of the strengths of social diversity and of the fact that community cohesion could not be achieved without effort. The participants agreed that Burnley was a town divided by class, ethnicity and religion and that these divisions were compounded by prejudice and fear. The participants felt that with more attention to curriculum planning, faith partnerships could contribute something of value to schools and colleges in the hope that young people would come to regard religious diversity as a feature of a tolerant pluralistic society.

It might also be worth noting that in this group, it was the Christian participants who had attended faith schools who had had the least contact with Muslims. This was not to say that they had no knowledge of other religious beliefs (they had, in fact, studied the basic principles of Christianity, Islam and Judaism when they were at school), but that they had attended schools in which there had been no Muslim pupils. This meant that whatever knowledge of religious diversity these young people had received at school, their *experience* of this diversity had been minimal. While this does not in itself present a case for the abolition of faith schools, it does call into question the extent to which mono-faith mono-cultural establishments are able to support the work of faith partnerships in multicultural towns and cities. The participants all believed that mono-cultural schools had as much responsibility for ensuring that their curriculum reflected British diversity as multicultural schools.

The final group of participants approached the activity by posing the question: What have faith groups done so far to unite the people of Burnley? Like the previous three groups, these participants were aware of the long history of religious and ethnic segregation in the town and that interfaith dialogue was a relatively new phenomenon. One of the participants made the suggestion that the most successful of these initiatives had been the two feasts hosted by the Christian and Muslim communities and that these celebratory events were an excellent way of uniting religious groups. The participants felt, however, that faith communities must work hard not to weaken the spiritual profile of the borough by forming ineffectual alliances with secular bodies. The two Muslim participants believed that although faith communities could bring their spiritual perspectives to bear on secular society, religious leaders needed to be more active if they were to avoid weakening their mission.

The group went on to discuss the contribution that the new Sixth Form faith centre could make to Burnley once the new schools were established.[9] The faith centre would be situated in a designated area of the Sixth Form and would be run by a newly appointed faith co-ordinator. At the time of the conference, the faith centre was being publicized as a spiritual focal point, the main purpose of which was to encourage different faith and non-faith communities to share the same space. The group felt that with enough enthusiasm, the faith centre would play an instrumental role in promoting religious cohesion and that in time, it would come to be seen as a place of peace and reconciliation.

The workshop activities described in this section provided the Spirit of Burnley participants with an opportunity to explore the similarities and differences between their religious traditions. This was probably the first time the participants had ever voiced their religious views in an interactive setting. The evaluation data collected the following day suggested that this had been a successful conference for all 16 recruits. The conference had heightened the Christian participants' awareness of the fact that behind hijabs and other Islamic symbols were real human experiences and deep religious conviction. For the Muslims, the testimonies of the Christian participants revealed that faith among the younger generations of the indigenous majority was not completely dead and that the emptying of church pews did not necessarily mean that religious beliefs had been abandoned. The recognition of different types of religious devotion that these activities had awakened created a climate in which serious dialogue could now begin.

As far as the achievement of the URI's own objectives was concerned, the group workshops were as timely as they were productive. The small size of the cohort had turned out to be advantageous in that by the end of the culture share activity, the participants knew each other by name and had learnt something about each individual contributor. This would have been more difficult to achieve with a larger group of people. By the time the workshops had begun, the participants had become better acquainted and a degree of trust had been established. By dividing the cohort in to groups of equal sizes, the facilitators had taken sufficient steps to ensure that everyone could contribute to the discussions.

There were several issues emerging from the workshops that make for interesting reflection. One of the most noteworthy observations was the remarkable degree of unanimity between the two faith communities. This can be attributed to the fact that, like some of the approaches described in the previous chapter, the discussions revolved around humanitarian themes rather than religious doctrines. The workshop objectives were defined in a way that would encourage rather than inhibit dialogue – an essential condition for community cohesion. The participants emphasized the *application* of faith rather than religious conviction and more than half expressed concerns about the failure of religious leaders to engage with young people. This was not because the participants did not recognize the value of leadership, but rather that they felt that priests and imams often preached from ivory towers and did not fully understand the challenges of living in a segregated town. Whatever truth there might be in these claims, policy makers would do well to involve religious clerics in strategic planning.

Despite the participants' disquiet about religious leaders, there was greater homogeneity among the Muslims than the Christians. There are a number of possible explanations for this. First, although it would be wrong to suggest that there are no sectarian divisions within Islam, there is greater doctrinal unity both nationally and internationally within Muslim communities. Among this group of young people alone, all nine Muslim participants belonged to the Sunni tradition while the seven Christians were affiliated to four different denominations. Second, most of the Muslim participants were of Pakistani heritage and had been reared in families where faith had been a central part of their daily lives. These similarities in religious tradition, ethnic group heritage and family influence go some way to explaining the cohesion within the group. Third, it is likely that the bipolar nature of Burnley and the segregation with which it had become associated had had a strong impact on the religious identities of the Muslim participants resulting in a uniformity that was missing among their Christians counterparts. Finally, it is possible that even for Muslims as moderate as these, world events such as the war in Iraq and the invasion of Afghanistan had created a strong sense of religious unity and that the conference provided a forum in which this unity could be expressed. It should not be forgotten, however, that religious conviction is diverse and subjective and the very small number of Muslims who attended the conference did not nearly reflect the heterogeneity of faith revealed in other parts of my research.

The ideas that ensued from the conference owed much to the involvement of the participants in other voluntary projects. Most of the suggestions that emerged from the discussions reflected the participants' concerns about the failure of faith communities to form partnerships with other voluntary and statutory organizations. While the participants made little reference to BBB or to the representation of faith groups on local authority committees, they were generally sanguine about the potential of religious bodies to contribute something of value to the wider society. Despite the differences in religious membership within the cohort, there was a high degree of consensus about how this could be achieved. Though the participants made little reference to the mundane administrative tasks in which voluntary groups were engaged (the preparation of funding proposals, taxation issues, strategic planning, evaluation and so forth), they were acutely aware of ethnic group divisions within the borough and of the weakening local and national religious landscape. The participants remembered vividly the disturbances of 2001 and expressed serious concerns about the growing support for the British National Party.

The issue now was not so much whether these young people had the will to implement changes but what kind of changes needed to be made.

BITING THE BULLET: SPONTANEOUS INTERFAITH DIALOGUE

Before going on to discuss the exhibition launch, there is one other feature of the Spirit of Burnley conference that is worthy of mention and that will be remembered by all the participants; namely, the opportunity to share religious views through informal discussion. While this was not something that had been scheduled into the programme, it turned out to be every bit as productive as the structured activities. In the initial stages of planning, the participants had requested that the Saturday evening be left free for social interaction or for people to organize their own entertainment as they wished.

At the end of dinner, the participants made their way into the lounge for an evening of relaxation. On entering the lounge, people helped themselves to tea and coffee and began to circulate. After 20 minutes or so of informal conversation, one of the project organizers instigated a discussion about the capacity building potential of religious communities at local and global levels. What began as a general exchange of ideas about religion and world peace soon escalated into a lively debate. Within a matter of minutes, the participants found that they were becoming increasingly polarized. One Muslim participant began to present his own analysis of the history and evolution of events in Palestine – a perspective that provoked strong reaction from some of the Christians. The debate might well have taken a different form had there been a presence of Jewish participants, but this scenario demonstrates the potential of interfaith events to rouse controversial issues and to allow adversarial views to be aired between members of different religious communities. More importantly, it challenges the view that interfaith dialogue can only be effective if differences are ignored and that any attempt to address emotive issues will inevitably result in conflict.

In due course and in accordance with more conventional interfaith approaches, the discussion moved away from geo-political events towards religious doctrines. It was clear that the participants were now acquiring the confidence to witness their faith in a mixed environment and to challenge the beliefs of others in a spirit of friendship. For the next three hours, the participants discussed the relationship between religion and civil law, the role of prophets in sacred texts, human creation, homosexuality, the Day of Judgement, salvation and everlasting life. The significance and interpretation of biblical and koranic edicts for twenty-first century Britain was central to most of the discussion and the participants were able to recognize similarities and differences between their respective theologies. There were, however, points of disagreement within as well as between the two faith groups, particularly on the issue of sexual morality.

As one might expect, the issue of homosexuality aroused strong controversy. Around half the Muslims agreed, for example, that while gay people existed in Muslim communities, homosexual relationships were contrary to Islamic teachings and could in no way be regarded as an acceptable alternative to heterosexual marriage. There was, however, an element of uncertainty among the remaining Muslims who felt that there was widespread ignorance within their own community of how people come to acquire their sexual orientation and that a growing number of Muslim scholars were beginning to consider new interpretations of koranic injunctions. The Christian participants, on the other hand, were more agreed that loving homosexual relationships between committed partners did not contravene biblical teachings and that if Christ were to return to the modern world, he would regard faithful relationships between gay people as morally acceptable. I was also struck by the fact that even those Christian participants who were affiliated to the more conservative denominations espoused relatively liberal views.

Although there were any number of issues that could, had time allowed, exposed differences in beliefs between the two communities, the opportunity for these participants to engage in serious debate in a neutral environment undoubtedly raised awareness and understanding. The participants were clearly able to identify some common ground in their religious traditions and even where they were unable to agree, they did at least demonstrate a willingness to accept a different version of reality. This suggests that the main strength of interfaith dialogue is not so much its ability to create doctrinal agreement (desirable though this would be), but to enable people from different faith communities to talk across religious divides. With skilful facilitation, an exercise of this nature can be a useful vehicle for challenging myths and misconceptions that have been internalized over a long period of time.

BUILDING CAPACITY

The two main tasks for the final day of the conference were: first, to make some provisional plans for the Spirit of Burnley exhibition and second, to complete the weekend with an interfaith celebration. Although the participants recognized that the activities of the previous 2 days had revealed some important similarities and differences, all claimed to have acquired more knowledge of each other's religious beliefs in this one weekend than they had achieved throughout the whole of their lives. From this point of view, it seemed that the first of the two main objectives of the project – to create a better understanding of different faith perspectives – had been met.

The second objective – to raise awareness of the contribution of faith groups to the local community – could not be fully assessed until after the exhibition had been launched and toured. The participants had, however, used the workshops as an opportunity to consider how their religious beliefs were of benefit to others and to reflect on the meaning of faith in their own lives. What transpired from these discussions, particularly for the Muslim participants, was that religious conviction and religious contribution went hand in hand. To show by good example was, *ipso facto*, living out one's faith in a way that would aid religious cohesion. All the participants expressed a willingness to work together in pursuit of a better world and in the first instance, this meant relaying the success of their project to local people.

The activities for Sunday began with an address by one of the facilitators. The address centred on the exhibition and the form that this should take. The participants were divided into three groups, each with its own rapporteur and a designated space in which to brainstorm ideas. The three groups made a list of exhibition suggestions which the rapporteurs summarized on flip charts. After 20 minutes of deliberation, the groups reconvened in the lounge to collate their suggestions. The participants had discussed a number of ways of launching their project, each of which would appeal to different audiences. Suggestions included a live performance, a static display, a DVD, a photograph album, a teaching pack and an interactive exhibition. The facilitators decided that the best way to proceed was to ask each participant to vote for three of the six suggestions. Within 15 minutes, the voting was complete and exhibition format decided. The three most popular exhibition options were the DVD, the teaching pack and the interactive display. The participants formed three respective groups, each of which would take responsibility for preparing the exhibition materials over the course of the next few weeks.

Once the three groups had been established, the next task was to consider the overall purpose of the exhibition and to formulate some procedures. The Chief Executive and the project facilitators agreed that the best way forward was for the participants to work in teams. In the weeks to come, each team would hold its own meetings and prepare the materials for the exhibition launch. The facilitators stressed the importance of common presentation themes and agreed to hold their own meetings to ensure that deadlines were being met. With proposals in place, the three groups convened to prepare their work plans.

The final activity of the day was the interfaith celebration. Aside from the fact that this seemed to be the most appropriate way of ending the conference, the participants believed that it would have symbolic significance in that it would help seal the trust that they had tried to achieve. Having completed their draft exhibition plans, the Christian group began preparing a series of hymns, bible readings and homilies while the Muslim participants prepared Islamic poems, koranic readings and some short stories about the life of the prophet Muhammad. The celebration was, by anyone's standard, a success. This final hour of worship and reflection included music, bidding prayers, songs, stories, personal testimonies and an exchange of peace gestures. The celebration ended with a joint blessing.

The success of the celebration can be attributed not only to the careful preparation, but to the willingness of the two groups to enter unfamiliar territory. Mindful of each other's doctrinal differences, the participants who led prayers and presented readings were careful not to compromise the beliefs of the other faith community and approached the service as an opportunity to celebrate unity. The bidding prayers and petitions began or ended with the words: *We ask Almighty God to help us in our appeal for . . .* rather than: *We make this prayer through Christ our Lord* in an attempt to avoid exclusive Christian and Islamic sentiments. However different the content of this service might have appeared to the participants, there can be no doubt that it gave them a different experience of worship and enabled them to recognize the sincerity of other devotees. Of all the activities in which the participants had engaged throughout the weekend, this joint celebration was the one that stretched religious boundaries to their limit.

PREPARING THE EXHIBITION

Over the course of the next few weeks, the three groups held a series of meetings to plan their exhibition launch. The participants were keen to complete the project as soon as possible in order to sustain their momentum and to build on the success of the conference. During this preparation period, the group leaders met on a fortnightly basis to exchange ideas and to update each other on progress. These meetings provided a forum for the identification of common themes and the collation of information. After 2 or so months of preparation, the whole cohort met for the final time to discuss their exhibition launch.

The group leaders decided to use the themes of *past, present* and *future* to present a faith narrative to the audience. The group leaders encouraged the participants to use their materials interchangeably when touring their exhibition around local schools, colleges, community centres, places of worship and other public places. The task now was to undertake whatever work was necessary to complete the remaining objectives of the project and for the groups to operationalize their work plans.

The group responsible for the interactive display purchased a large folding panel that divided into four sections. The participants agreed that since this was essentially a visual item, the most appropriate materials would be photographs, spiritual icons, magnetic objects, illustrations from religious publications, news stories and other resources that could be used to raise awareness of how the two main faith communities had evolved in the borough. After several meetings, one of the participants suggested that the best way of presenting the material would be to adopt a spiritual metaphor. It was decided that the metaphor of a tree would serve this purpose since it symbolized energy, nourishment and growth. The different parts of the tree would be used to illustrate the three exhibition themes with the roots representing the past, the trunk the present and the branches and leaves the future.

The participants designed a vertical display board which presented a historical narrative of the religious diversity of their town. After some discussion, it was decided that each member would take responsibility for a different section of the display. The final product comprised items of religious memorabilia, photographs of the town's oldest places of worship, biographical details of Christian and Muslim leaders, a selection of newspaper cuttings narrating the success of the interfaith feasts, a collage depicting the achievements of the BBB partnership and a large array of magnetic objects. The participants' intention was to depict faith as a life journey and to emphasize the concept of unity in diversity. On either side of the display was a whiteboard which the participants agreed would make a useful interactive aid.

The group responsible for the production of the DVD presented the themes of past, present and future through video footage and short stories. The participants conducted a number of live interviews with members of different faith communities and used these to produce a mini documentary which they called *The Best Street in the World* – a fictitious story of a neighbourhood that lived in harmony despite national, cultural and religious differences. The aim of the DVD was to present a positive view of religious and cultural diversity and to use modern genres to capture the interest of the audience. The final production included rap music, dramatized sketches and a futuristic vision of a world devoid of bigotry and prejudice. The group hoped to produce multiple copies of the DVD for circulation in schools, community centres and places of worship.

Like the DVD team, the participants responsible for the production of the teaching pack consulted regularly with the other two groups (particularly the group that had prepared the interactive display) in order to create a product that was compatible with the other exhibition materials. This group was aware of the challenges that teachers faced in promoting cultural and religious unity in Burnley, but hoped that the restructuring of secondary education would present new opportunities for including religious cohesion initiatives in the curriculum. Since one of the project facilitators (a former RE teacher) was already a salaried employee of BBB with a responsibility for managing a team of educational outreach workers, it seemed appropriate that she would lead the group in preparing a resource pack that could be used by local teachers to deliver Citizenship and/or Religious Education. The group made an additional effort to ensure that the resources reflected local issues with which school pupils would be familiar. Mindful of the busy workloads of teachers and of the monumental educational changes that were taking place in the town, the participants agreed that the resource pack should offer teachers the option of using the contents as teaching aids or of inviting the participants into the schools as guest speakers.

The teaching pack contained a large selection of note sheets and activities and a copy of the DVD produced by the second group. The note sheets and activities contained information about the local and global evolution of different faith communities and how religious beliefs come to be associated with particular ethnic groups. The group suggested that in addition to distributing these materials around the Burnley schools, a copy of the teaching pack should be kept in the recently established Sixth Form faith centre. Since the faith centre was intended as a facility for the whole community (including primary and secondary schools), the group felt that the teaching pack would be a useful resource for religious cohesion activities for young people.

By the spring of 2006, the three sub-groups had completed their exhibition tasks. A final meeting took place to discuss the presentation of the exhibition and to allocate responsibilities to key individuals. The meeting was also used to plan the exhibition tour and to consider other ways in which the participants could relay what they had learnt from their project.

THE EXHIBITION LAUNCH

The exhibition was launched at the Burnley Youth Theatre on a warm spring day. The venue was booked some six weeks prior to the event and a large number of stakeholders and well-known public figures were invited. These included the Mayor and Mayoress of Burnley, the leaders of all the local churches and mosques, representatives of organizations such as Burnley Borough Council, Burnley Action Partnership, BBB, East Lancashire Together[10] and a large number of other public and voluntary sector agencies. The event was publicized through newsletters, leaflets and the local media. The venue (designed for theatrical performances) was situated approximately one mile from the town centre. The event was attended by 78 people, all of whom were asked to complete an evaluation questionnaire at the end of the launch.[11]

The exhibition was presented by 10 of the 16 participants. The presentation began with some sound and light effects, a demonstration of different prayer positions and the lighting of candles. On lighting their candles, the participants uttered the words 'spiritual diversity is a blessing, not a threat' and united to form a semi-circle across the stage. The participants then revealed the first of their exhibition products – the interactive display – from behind the curtain. The participants spoke about the themes of past, present and future and explained how these themes had been incorporated into the exhibition products. To accompany their display, the participants produced a commentary book, a treasure chest and a box of children's items.

The next stage of the exhibition involved the presentation of the DVD. This contained video footage of different places of worship and commentaries of faith representatives. The theme of the past was depicted through a series of interviews, the first of which was with a Roman Catholic priest who talked about the history of the Catholic Church in Burnley from the period of the Reformation. Attention then turned to the Muslim community through a series of interviews with some of the first migrants from Pakistan who had settled in the UK during the 1960s. The interviewees described the circumstances that led to their settlement (including their hopes and aspirations) before going on to discuss their working lives in the textile and engineering industries. The interview section ended with one of the project facilitators talking about her memories of church festivals and Sunday school activities in the mid-1950s.

The theme of the present was encapsulated through biographical material that focused on the part that faith continued to play in people's lives. This section of the DVD highlighted the changing composition of local Roman Catholic and Anglican churches and explained how the recent influx of Eastern Europeans, Philippinos and South Indians had impacted on community relations in the borough. A group of Muslims then talked about their religious identities and how their faith impacted on their working lives. This provided the backdrop for the final theme – hope for the future.

The future of faith in Burnley was depicted through a short children's performance (referred to above as *The Best Street in the World*) of an imaginary world in which people from all walks of life shared the same neighbourhood. The sketch was produced by an after-school drama club that attracted teenagers from some of Burnley's most deprived wards. The aim of the drama was to synthesize the future hopes of children with those of the participants and to use the ideas from both groups as a way of promoting the project.

In the final part of the launch, the participants responsible for the education pack talked about the relevance of the project to the school curriculum. Some attempt was made to demonstrate the links between the three exhibition products and the group explained how the teaching materials could be adapted to meet the demands of different educational sectors and different subject syllabuses. Since the project was aimed at young people, the participants hoped that their exhibition would appeal to school children who may become involved in similar initiatives in the future.

TOURING THE EXHIBITION

The presence of teachers and clergy at the exhibition launch presented the participants with an opportunity to network their project and to attract the interest of other stakeholders. Within a few weeks of the exhibition launch, the participants had prepared a list of schools, public libraries, places of worship, community centres and other local agencies that they thought might be willing to host a Spirit of Burnley event. Once the list had been finalized, the group re-convened at Whalley Abbey to plan their tour. It was decided that the Sixth Form faith centre would provide a useful base for the planning and co-ordination of future interfaith initiatives. By the end of the summer, the project facilitators had received invitations to present their exhibition at the Burnley Community Festival, the central library, the East Lancashire Together convention, three local churches and several community centres. The extent to which the participants would be able to raise the profile of faith throughout the borough would, however, be the real proof of the pudding.

Some reflections

Until the formation of BBB in 2001, there was little evidence of Christian–Muslim dialogue in Burnley (a consequence of ethnic segregation that began in the 1960s) and no serious attempt to unite people from different faith communities. The event at Whalley Abbey can be seen as an achievement on the part of young people who recognized the importance of religious cohesion in segregated English towns and whose parents had never managed to question their own cultural and religious perspectives. In this sense, the URI can be seen as an opportunity for young people to address social divisions that have taken root in the UK over several decades. With sufficient planning, these initiatives could help remove cultural as well as religious barriers and achieve many of the objectives of Citizenship Education.

The evidence suggests that although the URI conference was only one element of the Spirit of Burnley project, its strengths outweighed its weaknesses. The conference owed much of its success to the fact that the participants were allowed to set their own agenda and address what they saw as important community issues. Although the project attracted only a small number of recruits, all had different experiences of religious socialization and were at different stages of personal development. The following comments (taken from the conference evaluation questionnaires) offer some insights into what the participants felt they had learnt from the residential weekend:

I have learnt more about the Christian faith and about things that are very common with Islam. The differences that exist are very small. I have learnt that Christians place a high emphasis on moral laws. (male Muslim aged 18 years)

There has been an open forum of discussion which has allowed me to learn more about my own faith and that of my Muslim friends. The use of discussion and workshops has made me realize how close the Christian and Muslim faiths are to one another. (male Christian aged 22 years)

I have had the opportunity to meet with and speak to people of the same faith as me and those of a different faith which has helped to develop my understanding and knowledge both of my own faith and the Christian faith. We have many many similarities. (female Muslim aged 23 years)

I have learnt that although our religions may be different, there are some very strong similarities – essentially, our deep desire to be good people and to love and serve God. The differences in worship were interesting, especially as I had little knowledge of certain areas and issues – the treatment of women, violence, fundamentalism, terrorism, homophobia etc – but I had a chance to discuss these issues at length. Although I do not understand fully, I can respect differences and feel I know more. (female Christian aged 18 years)

I have learnt that Muslims and Christians dialogue with each other most effectively through the developments of debate. That is to say, the more we practice talking to each other, the easier it will be to enter into dialogue in the future. I think this is facilitated because of our development in understanding the other. (female Muslim aged 24 years)

I have learnt a massive amount about the Muslim faith and an understanding that our faiths are more similar than I thought. A sense of unity with my Muslim brothers and sisters has been a definite personal growth. (female Christian aged 22 years)

Though these comments are encouraging, the participants did express concerns about the itinerary of the weekend and the limited faith community representation. Seven of the participants commented on the absence of Hindus, Sikhs and Buddhists whom they felt would have enlivened the conference. These critics did, however, acknowledge that the conference had provided an excellent forum for interfaith dialogue and for the discussion of political issues that had a religious dimension. The second criticism was that the itinerary had been a little ambitious and that there was insufficient time to explore some of the issues to their full potential. Four of the participants felt that this could have been avoided by a smaller number of planned activities and more detailed attention to the main themes.

Despite the relatively small cohort, the balance of ethnic, gender and religious profiles reflected the composition of the borough. The failure of the project to attract people from faith communities other than Christian and Muslim was undoubtedly due to the general lack of religious activity among young people within the town and to the exclusive nature of certain religious groups. The question of how to encourage members of fringe organizations (Mormons, Jehovah's Witnesses, Evangelicals and Pentecostalists, for example; all of whom were active in the town) to partake in interfaith initiatives is particularly challenging.

The identification of common religious values enabled the participants to consider new ways of raising the profile of faith in secular contexts. Since over half the participants (nine in all) were employed either as youth workers or project leaders, the opportunity to promote religious issues through work activities presented itself more readily than might otherwise have been the case. Moreover, although these nine participants worked in secular environments (with the exception of a young woman who was employed by the Lancashire Council of Mosques), their identification of humanitarian principles had, according to the questionnaire data, provided them with some new ideas about how to embed religious concepts such as integrity, compassion, generosity and self-sacrifice into the workplace. Examples of these included the promotion of social justice through equal opportunities policies (achieved in some working contexts through the implementation of Fair Trade policies), generosity through charity donations and reconciliation and forgiveness through conflict resolution.

The participants suggested a number of ways in which they could contribute as a faith partnership to the development of public services. The tendency of local authorities to allow community groups to oversee their own affairs, however, means that the opportunities for voluntary organizations to contribute to statutory provision are limited. With the exception of chaplaincy services in hospitals, faith communities play a peripheral role in the NHS and there is little funding available for the inclusion of faith-based initiatives in other health organizations. Furthermore, the Health Service presents fewer opportunities for religious cohesion activities than the voluntary sector and the education system.

Education is the one public service in which faith partnerships can compensate for the alleged failure of religious leaders to capture the interest of school and college students. My research confirms that young people of school age embrace religious issues from a wide range of perspectives and that this heterogeneity is widespread even among believers themselves. While it would be premature to suggest that religious leadership is redundant in the lives of *all* young people, the challenges for faith leaders working in educational contexts should not be underestimated. Faith schools are acutely aware of the difficulties of formulating overtly doctrinal mission statements in their attempt to instil religious values into students and school chaplains are having to think long and hard about the ways in which they approach their ministry. As far as Christianity is concerned, it is patently clear that the church has lost an unprecedented amount of influence in Britain and that few young people from Christian backgrounds attend church or Sunday school. While second and subsequent Muslims continue to express their identities in religious terms, they too are showing signs of fragmentation. At present, there is much discussion among Muslim leaders about how to engage with young people and of the implications of western secularization for the future of Islam.

The fact that the Spirit of Burnley participants were themselves young adults who claimed to have learnt so much from each other suggests that religious cohesion in multicultural, multifaith schools and colleges is still worthy of pursuit. If Religious and/or Citizenship Education are to have any real impact on this agenda, one of the best ways forward in the current climate is to allow groups of young outreach workers to play a more active role in the curriculum. As far as the Spirit of Burnley project was concerned, all three exhibition products were likely to appeal to school pupils, not only because the material contained modern media images, but because it was young people themselves who were involved in the initiative. Moreover, many of the themes of Citizenship

Education (liberty, democracy, human rights, individual freedom, respect for diversity and so forth) lend themselves to the objectives of religious cohesion and to the more general principles on which faith partnerships are founded.

While it would be unrealistic to suggest that experiential initiatives such as the Spirit of Burnley project will appeal to anything other than a small number of religious enthusiasts, the potential for these initiatives to contribute to community cohesion in areas of the UK that are affected by civil unrest should not be underestimated. From the outset, the participants were clear that their two main objectives were to improve people's understanding of faith and to raise awareness of what faith communities could contribute to the wider society. Like the educational outreach approaches described in Chapter 3, this was an exercise involving the identification of common values and the dissemination of information rather than proselytization and recruitment. The ultimate test of initiatives such as these, however, will be the participants' ability to persuade school and college students, public sector workers, community groups and civic leaders of the importance of religious cohesion in times of conflict.

One initiative, two approaches

My research unearthed some significant differences in the ways in which the same interfaith initiative – The Spirit of the North – was launched in two East Lancashire towns between 2005 and 2006. The purpose of this summary is not to reiterate the strengths and weaknesses of the two projects, but to offer a comparative analysis of how the main principles of the United Religions Initiative were put into practice once the participants had been recruited. The discussion is intended to highlight the strategies that were adopted by the project leaders and to demonstrate the ways in which interfaith activities can be tailored to meet the needs of different groups of people. The analysis should aid our understanding of how the principles of religious cohesion can be applied in both secular and sacred contexts.

The ethnic and religious profiles of Blackburn and Burnley were remarkably similar. Despite variations in belief, Christians and Muslims represented the two main faith groups of the towns, followed by a much smaller number of Hindus, Buddhists, Jews and Sikhs. The main purpose of the URI workshops was to unite young people from different religious backgrounds and to support them in preparing an exhibition. In Blackburn, the approach that was adopted was a secular one with faith as a subliminal element; while in Burnley, the activities were faith-oriented, but the exhibition was interactive rather than photographic. Though the religious identities of the Burnley participants were more clearly defined, the two projects convey equally effective ways of achieving the same objectives.

The Spirit of Burnley project echoes the *experiential* model of religious cohesion described in Chapter 1. This is an approach that invites participants to take part in activities that nurture religious empathy. This strategy assumes that participants are essentially people of faith who are willing to learn about other belief systems through action-based workshops. Broadly speaking, this was what the Burnley cohort managed to achieve. The residential conference presented an opportunity not only for dialogue, but for participation and interaction. An approach such as this will stretch religious boundaries without encroaching on the rights of individuals. In addition to interfaith workshops, experiential activities include feasts and celebrations, pilgrimages and retreats, visits to holy places, charity events, educational initiatives and, most ambitious of all, joint worship.

Another important feature of the experiential model is the value it places on personal exploration. Experiential strategies work best when people are prepared to move away from the environments in which they live and work and convene in neutral spaces. Only then are participants able to step out of their comfort zones and embrace difference – an experience that can evoke feelings of vulnerability and cause the individual to question, perhaps for the first time, his or her internalized version of reality. For those who are secure in their spirituality but eager to learn more about other systems of belief, initiatives of this kind may do little more than affirm religious identity. On the other hand, those who are less sure of their convictions may find that an experiential programme provides them with answers to searching questions – an experience that could even lead to a religious conversion. This did not, however, occur at Whalley Abbey. Although the participants met on neutral ground and claimed to have learnt quite a lot about each other's beliefs, there were few groundbreaking changes.

The Spirit of Blackburn exemplifies a different religious cohesion model than the Spirit of Burnley. The recruitment of young people from mainly secular backgrounds presented a greater challenge to the project leaders than would have been the case had the participants expressed an interest in interfaith dialogue. Here, the project needed to be presented as a secular activity in the same way that it might be introduced in schools. Given that the participants were students of photography rather than members of religious communities, the philosophy of the URI needed to be incorporated into what was, to all intents and purposes, an educational assignment. By asking the students to take photographs of religious devotees in workplaces and other secular environments, the project leaders were advancing the notion that secular society is dependent on people of faith. This implicit rather than explicit reference to spirituality (rather than religion) echoes the contributory rather than the experiential model – an approach which aims to give faith communities a voice in an age of increasing religious indifference.

At this point, it is worth emphasizing that the three models I have described in this book – the dialogical, the experiential and the contributory – have equal value and that none of these is superior. In societies as diverse as the UK, religious cohesion strategies can be employed in different ways and must, if they are to have any serious impact, reflect the social and cultural dynamics of participatory groups. When Christian and Muslim leaders engage in dialogue, they will converse in a very different way from when they are invited to contribute to strategic planning meetings at the local Town Hall. Similarly, when teachers and project leaders are involved in the facilitation of religious activities for young people, they need to consider the profiles of the participants, the nature and extent of religious conviction and the availability of skills and resources. It should also be remembered that voluntary projects are, by their very nature, different from educational initiatives.

The Spirit of the North projects in Burnley and Blackburn make for an interesting comparative analysis. The Burnley participants used their project as an opportunity to learn more about each other's religious perspectives and to identify similarities and differences in their beliefs. This was made possible by the fact that the recruits were local residents who had witnessed civil conflict. It was their genuine concern for the future of their town that motivated them to prepare an exhibition that would emphasize the importance of ethnic and religious unity among other people with whom they came into contact. The Blackburn group, on the other hand, used a collection of photographs to depict religious diversity and to illustrate the contribution that faith communities make to secular society. *Prima facie*, the messages contained in these photographs were little more than the by-product of a college assignment, but for those interested in raising the profile of faith, it was an effective way of making young people aware of the significance of religious identity in a modern secular society. Both projects demonstrate different ways of promoting religious cohesion in diverse and challenging contexts.

Notes

1 Most of this funding has been provided by the Home Office and by individual donations.
2 Like most other community based initiatives, plans as ambitious as these require sustained funding. The URI executive committee estimated that between 2006 and 2009, the organization would require £250,000 per annum to bring its plans to bear.
3 These can include other religious groups, local councils, schools, colleges and civic centres.
4 Since the participants were already students of Photography, it was clear that many of the skill-building sessions had been unnecessary. This may help to explain the sporadic patterns of attendance.
5 A centre of peace and reconciliation established in 1993 a result of an IRA attack. The Blackburn participants presented their exhibition to an audience of civil servants, youth workers, religious leaders and representatives of the British Council.
6 Of the nine Muslim participants, five were male and four were female. The Christian group (three males and four females) included one Roman Catholic, one Anglican, one Methodist and four Baptists.
7 Several of the participants had been named after a grandparent or some other close relative.
8 Although there was general agreement among the Muslim participants that the structure and organization of modern secular employment did not always allow time for regular worship and that it made

fasting during Ramadan difficult, there was disagreement about the circumstances under which exceptions could be made.

9   The point has already been made that in September 2006, the eight high schools of Burnley closed and re-opened as five 'new' establishments. The new *Burnley Schools' Sixth Form* was established on one of the former high school sites.

10 An alliance of voluntary and community groups across four East Lancashire boroughs.

11 Of these 78 attendees, 67 completed questionnaires. These included 45 Christians, 14 Muslims and 8 people who identified themselves as having no faith.

5. Religious leadership in segregated towns: a changing landscape

Religiosity in Britain is complex and fast-changing. As church attendance fell into decline in the late-1960s and early-1970s, new forms of spirituality began to emerge, bringing with them a range of alternative expressions. At the same time, the settlement of BME communities from other areas of the global compass added to the diversity of the religious landscape, resulting in large numbers of people with different religious beliefs sharing the same (mainly urban) space. Whatever the sociological analysis of the current religious climate, the fact of this diversity is indisputable.

In the mill towns of northern England, the influx of several thousand migrant workers from India, Pakistan and Bangladesh (and more recently, from Eastern Europe) presented a new challenge to those involved in religious cohesion. The fact that religious convictions vary so much within as well as between these communities adds to the complexity. Teachers, religious leaders and project managers are acutely aware that while religious beliefs may be important to some social groups, there are countless numbers of people for whom it is insignificant, but who may, none the less, be willing to support the work of faith partnerships. How then can religious leaders exercise an influence over young people in ways that will improve community relations? How might these young people be brought together in something that can be called 'religious unity?' Who might be best suited to facilitate this endeavor? And what are the implications of this for conventional religious ministry?

My own research shows that if faith communities are to reach young people, they need to adapt to the social, economic and cultural changes that are shaping modern Britain. I should mention, however, that since the data contained in this book were collected in Burnley and Blackburn, it is Christian–Muslim relations that will receive the most attention. The leadership strategies I have described in this chapter were implemented during the second year of the investigation when Burnley was undergoing some major changes in service provision, particularly in education. The restructuring of the high schools and the opening of a new sixth form created a timely opportunity for members of faith groups – lay representatives as well as religious leaders – to contribute to the social and spiritual needs of the wider community.

The chapter is divided into three sections, the first of which concerns the representation of faith at local level. Consideration has been given to the role that faith communities play in local authority strategic planning and voluntary sector initiatives – issues that reflect the contributory model. The second section examines the attempts of Christian and Muslim leaders to engage in dialogue in the hope of learning more about each other's religious traditions and how to build an effective partnership. Despite the co-existence of these two faith communities in East Lancashire for several decades, it is only recently that religious leaders have begun to take an interest in each other's beliefs and to explore the possibility of working together – an endeavour that could almost certainly help to restore civil cohesion in segregated towns. In the final section, attention is given to new directions in religious leadership with regard to women and young people. The experiences of both these groups can be used to inform faith communities of what kind of leadership strategies work best and how these strategies might be used to support other initiatives. These issues have important implications for social policy and for the future direction of faith partnerships in the UK.

The representation of faith communities in civic renewal

Within the last decade, there has been a concerted effort on the part of faith communities to contribute to civic renewal. This effort has enabled public, private and voluntary sector agents to engage more openly with faith representatives and to include them in a range of community developments. The extensive research carried out by the Northwest Development Agency (2003) revealed high levels of regenerational activity among lay members of religious organizations, particularly in the more deprived parts of the UK where people are often disengaged from the political process. According to the survey, faith communities in the North West of England were actively involved in projects linked with homelessness, racism, crime, drug misuse, mental health and the environment. The survey also confirmed that people of faith were active deliverers of care services.

Slowly but surely, faith communities have started to engage more frequently with each other and to contribute to some innovative areas of government policy. Since the mid-1990s, regional faith forums have pursued representation on England's eight Regional Assemblies (Greater London operates, in effect, as a ninth, but with its own elected Mayor and Assembly), all of which work in consultation with national interfaith bodies.[1] At the time of writing, the Inter Faith Network for the United Kingdom (a registered charity established in 1987) was working to advance public knowledge and was the main forum through which these regional faith groups were able to convene. The Network had its own website[2] and published newsletters, annual reviews, directories of interfaith organizations and other materials. In 2003, the Network also established a Faith Communities Consultative Forum which aimed to facilitate national discussions on policy issues such as the prevention of terrorism,[3] racial and religious hatred, equality and human rights and, more recently, the restoration of community cohesion following the London bombings in July 2005. Faith groups around the country are now working more closely than ever before with uniformed services (particularly the Police), local councils, educational establishments and commercial organizations.

By 2007, BBB was represented on a number of local, regional and national bodies involved in civic renewal. These bodies included the Burnley Action Partnership, the Burnley Community Network, the Lancashire Council of Mosques, Churches Together in Lancashire, the Lancashire Advisory Committee on Religious Education and Collective Worship, the Lancashire and the North West Forums of Faith and the aforementioned Inter Faith Network for the United Kingdom. The organization also worked in partnership with a number of other voluntary groups including Breaking Barriers in Burnley,[4] the Burnley Youth Council, Burnley Lane Action Group, the Outreach and Development Agency of

Blackburn Cathedral, East Lancashire Together and the Council for Voluntary Service. It was through this network of voluntary and statutory organizations that BBB was able to contribute to the borough council's community cohesion strategy and the Lancashire County Council corporate plan.

The Burnley Action Partnership (BAP) was a coalition of representatives from local business groups, public sector agencies and voluntary organizations. The partnership (officially known as the Local Strategic Partnership) was established in 2002 as part of the government's Neighbourhood Renewal Strategy – a central directive in which 88 local authorities in England engaged with local stakeholders in policy formation and decision making. The Burnley Community Network (BCN) was established alongside the BAP with the aim of attracting a wider number of grass roots participants such as local residents, volunteers and members of disadvantaged groups. If all went to plan, this would increase participation and assist in the development and evaluation of new community initiatives. The Burnley, Pendle and Rossendale Council for Voluntary Service was responsible for overseeing the activities of the BCN and for ensuring fair participation and representation.

BBB made a significant contribution to the BAP community cohesion strategy, most of which was documented in the borough council's own literature. The 2-year strategic plan for 2005–2007 highlighted the importance of including churches and mosques in the pursuit of better community relations and the dissemination of positive messages about social diversity (Burnley Borough Council, 2005a). One of the main arguments in the plan was that if this could be achieved, the potential for the kind of conflict that had occurred in 2001 would be much reduced. Particular emphasis was placed on the neighbourhood location of the town's main places of worship and on the suggestion that community cohesion strategies that included the support of faith groups could help tackle social exclusion (ibid., p. 22). It was no coincidence that one of the two BBB centres (a Christian church hall) was located in the area in which the disturbances had broken out and where there had been a large amount of damage to properties. The other centre (a local mosque) was situated some three or four hundred yards away in the terraced streets of an Asian populated ward. BBB held its committee meetings at both these centres.

In a later section of the plan (ibid., p. 40), reference was made to the inclusion of community cohesion issues in the school/college curriculum – an appeal that was motivated by the belief that this would create an opportunity for BBB to contribute, directly or indirectly, to Citizenship and Religious Education and to some new developments that were about to be introduced by Lancashire County Council. The more general aim, however, was to involve BBB in the planning and organization of religious cohesion activities for the young people of Burnley – a timely prospect in the light of the restructuring of secondary education now underway. After some consultation between the Local Education Authority and a number of BBB representatives, a vision for the contribution of faith communities was agreed and a partnership between the two bodies established.

Another example of how BBB was able to contribute to the borough council's cohesion strategy was through a conflict resolution programme. In the autumn of 2005, an initiative known as *The Good Relations Project* was introduced in Burnley by Elevate East Lancashire – a government pathfinder organization responsible for ensuring fair access to housing and for building positive relations in towns and cities where housing regeneration was taking place. The aim of the project was to engage all sections of the community in the decision making process in the hope that this would strengthen local identity. A partnership between Burnley Borough Council and Elevate East Lancashire was established to help with the implementation of the BAP community relations plan. The Chief Executive of Elevate commissioned Mediation Northern Ireland (a neighbourhood renewal organization from Belfast) to offer advice and support to the partnership and to establish a forum for the formulation of effective peace strategies. A three year consultation programme was produced, the outcomes of which would be shared with all Elevate authorities and a number of other pathfinder organizations.

The Good Relations Project comprised a series of workshops convened by a sub-group of neighbourhood renewal advisors who were experienced in building good relations and tackling conflict. The workshops were entitled: *Social and Economic Change, Market Renewal, The Community Sector, Segregation, Identity* and *Civic Leadership*. Two representatives of BBB took part in the programme and assisted with the evaluation. The workshops provided a forum for BBB to disseminate information about some of the initiatives that were taking place in the town and to relay the outcomes of these initiatives to other stakeholders. Mediators from the Northern Ireland group facilitated the discussions and devised a framework for the aversion of conflict in the north of England.

The programme achieved three broad objectives. First, it provided an opportunity for representatives of local organizations to benefit from the experiences of people who had worked in some of the most challenging social and political contexts in the UK – contexts in which sporadic violence had damaged social relations. The second achievement was the programme's success in uniting community representatives who shared common goals. The programme had produced a network of activists who were able to promote local initiatives and who were keen to enter into new partnerships. The third and most important achievement was that the programme had created interactive opportunities for people who held profoundly different views on how a cohesive society could best be achieved. It was important, therefore, that the Good Relations participants convened in a space that was conducive to dialogue and where difficult conversations could take place.

The extent to which BBB was able to achieve the targets of the 2005–7 strategic plan and to develop the skills advanced by the Good Relations Project is not for discussion here. This section serves merely to offer some examples of policy initiatives to which faith communities are able to contribute and to identify possible future directions. It is worth reiterating, however, that if faith groups are to play a more active role in community relations, they will need to find new ways of working with secular bodies, for it is only by doing this that they will be able to increase their number of volunteers and win the support of religious sceptics. This is no mean feat. Faith communities in western societies have been driven (mainly by secular forces) to the margins of society where they are finding it increasingly difficult to attract anything other than a small number of enthusiasts. The challenge for faith partnerships is to retreat from their doctrinal positions and seek representation on this secular public platform.

Community cohesion strategies are challenging and ambitious. Council officers are spending an increasing amount of time tracking the progress of individual stakeholders and considering new applications for funding. Reluctant though they may be, those involved in organizing and facilitating religious projects must acquire greater levels of administrative competence if they are to build on their achievements and maximize their chances of public funding. The skills involved in identifying needs, defining objectives, establishing targets, outlining core activities, estimating costs, managing budgets, assessing risks and preparing evaluation reports mark an unwelcome change for most voluntary groups and a rather cynical attempt on the part of statutory bodies to hold the voluntary sector to account. But this is the direction in which faith communities will need to move if they are to achieve their full potential.

Unity between Christian and Muslim leaders

In the spring of 2006, BBB appointed its first leadership officer to encourage dialogue between Christian and Muslim clerics. By now, a number of interfaith initiatives had been launched in the town for which BBB had received a substantial amount of funding. It was clear, however, that most of these initiatives had been spearheaded by lay people (including a small number of paid officers) rather than priests and imams; hence, opportunities needed to be created for religious leaders to work together in response to the borough council's strategic plan. In the longer term, it was hoped that the newly appointed officer (a 0.3 fractional appointment for an initial period of 12 months) would establish close links with the young people's officer and the women's officer, both of whom were appointed around the same time on respective 0.4 and 0.3 contracts.

The main brief of the faith leadership officer was to evaluate existing interfaith provision and to build on what BBB had already been achieved. His principal aim was to enlist the support of churches and mosques in interfaith events and to facilitate at least one major activity before the end of the year. The view of BBB members was that if religious leaders could recognize the value of interfaith dialogue, unity between their respective communities would follow.

Within a few weeks of his appointment, the faith leadership officer helped to establish two committees; namely, a Christian–Muslim working party and an imams' forum. He then organized two events, both of which aimed to maximize the potential for faith leaders and lay people to form an integrated network and for the leaders themselves to establish a closer working relationship. The first event was a one day seminar entitled *Faith Leadership for a Better Burnley*. The event was intended as an opportunity for priests and imams to discuss their different approaches to leadership and to address some of the issues contained in the borough council's strategic plan. This would be the first time Christian and Muslim leaders had ever met to discuss faith relations in Burnley or how a faith partnership could be used to tackle other forms of social segregation. The event would also allow religious leaders to exchange information about their own communities and to identify common beliefs – a timely initiative given that BBB was now in the sixth year of its evolution and that a large number of civic renewal strategies had been implemented by other voluntary groups. The second event – a public seminar – took place some six weeks later and was extended to a wider audience. The purpose of this event was to relay some of what had been discussed at the faith leaders' seminar to a larger group of delegates including clerics from other towns, teachers, project leaders and lay people. This would enable Christian and Muslim leaders to discuss their respective beliefs in a more open forum in the hope that it might attract some local influential figures.

The *Faith Leadership for a Better Burnley* seminar was held on a weekday at the BBB mosque and attracted around twenty clerics. The itinerary began with joint scripture readings and a quiet time of prayer. This was followed by a series of in-depth discussions about community cohesion, clerical training, faith partnerships and religious education. In their discussion of cohesion issues, the participants suggested some possible strategies for dealing with segregation, civil disorder, religious extremism and racial intolerance in schools. They then attempted a scenario activity in which they were asked to consider how a faith partnership might respond to an act of terrorism in an English city and what they, the faith leaders could do to help prevent religious radicalization. Inevitably, this led to a discussion about stereotypes and about the role that priests and imams played in their own communities. There was concurrence within the group that rapprochement between religious leaders and secular authorities was essential if civil conflict was to be averted. The participants recognized that there was a large amount of work to be done within their own communities if religious cohesion was to be achieved and that Islam and Christianity presented different challenges. While it was felt that much more effort was needed at all levels if Christians and Muslims in the UK were to understand each other better, it was also acknowledged that differences between the two communities could not be ignored. For the Christian leaders, the greatest challenge was how to engage with young people whose perceptions of Christianity were largely negative; while for the imams, the overriding concern was how Islam could adapt to secular societies.

The second event – the public seminar – was held towards the end of the summer and convened by the Bishop of Burnley. Like the faith leaders' event, the seminar was held at the BBB mosque and attracted around 70 lay people. The event began with a twenty minute presentation by a local imam on the basic principles of Islam. A series of photographs were used to illustrate religious symbols, places of worship, pilgrimages and the Islamic dress code. The imam talked about the five pillars of Islam and the centrality of faith in the lives of Muslims. At the end of the address, the attendees were invited to ask questions and/or to comment on what they had heard. The imam responded to questions about self-denial (particularly fasting during the month of Ramadan), Muslim rites of passage, acts of charity, the concept of prayer, the role of women, animal sacrifice, alcohol consumption, halal food and, most controversial of all, the Sharia penal code. After half an hour or so of audience participation, a Roman Catholic priest was invited to the podium to present a Christian perspective.

The priest began his address by outlining the origin of the Christian church and its fragmentation throughout the centuries. This helped to contextualize the main differences between Trinitarian denominations and enabled the Muslim attendees to understand the evolution of Christianity. The priest then focused on Christian doctrines such as the virgin birth, the deity of Christ, the trinity, the resurrection, life after death, sin, suffering, atonement, grace and forgiveness. Throughout his address, the priest used a number of religious aids including a Bible, a crucifix, a bottle of holy water, a missal, some rosary beads, a holy picture, a hymn book and a copy of the divine office. Although most of these objects were associated with Roman Catholicism, it was clear that the priest's main objective was to highlight the importance of symbolism in religious expression and to draw some parallels between the two traditions. The priest then regaled the audience with a story of a visit that he and his parishioners had made to a local mosque as part of a BBB initiative some months earlier. These parishioners had expressed some initial apprehension about the visit and were unsure of what to expect. The priest went on to explain how, once they had entered the mosque and removed their shoes, the visitors began to ask questions about Islamic worship and to identify similarities between their own faith (most notably, the significance of prayer beads and holy books) and that of their Muslim counterparts. Despite their awareness of differences between the two traditions, it seemed that the visit had been successful in helping these Christian visitors to overcome their fear of difference.

It would, of course, be wrong to suggest that religious differences can be quickly resolved or that people are equally willing to embrace change. However welcoming a faith community might be to those who hold different beliefs, religious prejudices are deeply internalized, particularly in segregated towns. In Burnley, unity between the two main faith communities only really began in 2001 (after almost 40 years of Christian–Muslim co-existence) and the faith leaders' consortium was established even later than this. The next decade or so will reveal whether or not religious leaders will have any real impact on faith relations in Burnley and the direction that these relations should take. In the meantime, religious leaders need to consider the effectiveness of their ministry and to explore new ways of working together if positive community relations are to be achieved. Those leaders most willing to enter into partnership with other voluntary groups and local service providers will almost certainly have an impact. In a pluralistic society in which people from different religious, ethnic and cultural backgrounds live in close proximity, this will be a challenging but critical endeavour.

New directions in religious leadership

In mixed communities, religious leadership is a rapidly changing phenomenon. While the main purpose of the investigation was to explore the effectiveness of religious cohesion strategies in Burnley and Blackburn, I also became involved (rather by default) in the evaluation of some innovative strategies adopted by BBB and the Development Agency of Blackburn Cathedral between 2005 and 2007 – strategies that had national as well as local implications. The data contained in this section derive from a variety of sources including in-depth interviews with members of faith communities (particularly religious leaders, lay people and project managers), fieldwork notes taken at meetings and ethnographic observations of a number of interfaith events. Much of these data reflect the hopes and aspirations of people living in East Lancashire at the time of my research. What follows should be of interest not only to those involved in the facilitation of interfaith and/or community cohesion initiatives, but to academics (particularly social scientists) concerned with the issue of religious identity.

YOUNG PEOPLE SPEAK OUT: ATTITUDES
TOWARDS RELIGIOUS LEADERS

One of the most significant if not particularly surprising research findings was the variation in religious conviction between Christians and Muslims. I have already made the point that Muslims from virtually every generation are more likely to hold religious beliefs and to engage in religious practices than non-Muslims. The exceptions, however, are too important to be ignored. It should not be forgotten that it was Christian representatives who were instrumental in the formation of the first faith partnerships in Burnley and Blackburn and who initiated the process of Christian–Muslim dialogue. Some of these activists were leaders of Christian denominations (including ordained clergy), while others were ordinary church-goers involved in a number of voluntary and community projects. For Christian people such as these, the pursuit of religious cohesion is part and parcel of loving one's neighbour and of striving to make the world a better place.

Despite these laudable efforts, the fact remains that it tends to be people of middle age and above who are involved in most of these activities. Within the first few months of my fieldwork, it was clear that if religious cohesion was to be achieved in East Lancashire, there was a very real need for religious leaders and other representatives to engage with young people and to build capacity in a wider range of social contexts. This realization came from the understanding that people in their teens, twenties and thirties were no longer expressing their religious convictions through regular church/mosque attendance and that religious clerics were having difficulty in reaching younger groups. While religious beliefs continue to be an important part of identity for British Muslims, there is a substantial amount of evidence to suggest that youth workers, sports leaders and project managers are having a greater influence over second and subsequent generation members than imams and other religious leaders. Added to this is the fact that Muslim women have, for cultural rather than religious reasons, always been less visible in mosques than their male counterparts.

For the so-called 'Christian' population, the situation is more complex. For better or worse, church-going has become something of an anachronism in the UK and there are few signs of a revival. Moreover, the majority of those who have had some former association with Christianity (through baptism or confirmation, for example) know little about other religious communities and show minimal interest in interfaith dialogue. The diminishing number of worshippers in mainstream congregations – a consequence both of the weakening of traditional religious authority and the rejection of divine revelation – has made the role of Christian leaders more precarious than ever before. The current picture is one of diminution and uncertainty, with disparate levels of religious conviction within as well as between Christian denominations. If faith communities are to have any real chance of working together to achieve a sense of common purpose, religious leaders will need to grapple with these changes and find new ways of reaching young people.

There are several factors that can shape the attitudes of younger generations of Christians towards religious leaders. In western democracies, the rise of media technology, the erosion of time-honoured institutions such as the extended family and the seemingly irreversible acceleration of secular consumerism are among the arguments advanced by sociologists of religion for falling (mainstream) church attendance and the weakening of Christian leadership. In contrast, the revival of more intense forms of Christianity (most notably, Pentecostalism and conservative Evangelicalism) and the endurance of non-Christian faiths, all of which continue to attract young people, can be seen as a rejection of secular modernity among those who hold on to religious hope. In the last analysis, it will be the ability of faith leaders to respond to these changing forms of religious expression and to the challenges posed by secularization that could have the biggest impact on future faith relations.

The school survey which my colleagues and I administered in East Lancashire in the summer of 2006 revealed strikingly different attitudes between Christians and Muslims towards religious authority. The main findings are worth reiterating. The most significant difference was the greater degree of respect among Muslim pupils for religious clerics – a result that was attributable not only to differences in religious conviction but to religious influences outside school. The fact that mosque attendance was more common than church attendance was indicative not only of strong parental influence but of the greater cohesion of Muslim communities. By comparison, the religious indifference of Christian pupils (or to be more precise, pupils who defined themselves as Christian) and their limited contact with priests and/or ministers reflected a largely secular attitude and a decline in deference towards Christian clergy. While neither the strong religious beliefs of the Muslim respondents nor their commitment to mosque attendance should be taken at face value, the different degrees of religious activity between the two communities go some way towards explaining these pupils' attitudes towards religion. The extent to which religious leaders are able to change these attitudes is, of course, another matter.

Though they produce illuminating data, social surveys such as these should be treated with caution. For one thing, it is difficult to measure the effects of religious leadership on young people when there are so many other influences at work; and for another, there is no knowing whether respect for religious authority is something younger generations (particularly young Muslims) feel they *ought* to show. The following interview comments offer some insights into the perceived role and status of imams through the eyes of three young Muslim men:

I don't attend mosque like I used to. We attended mosque when we were young, but I've been to university since then and that really broadens your horizons . . . you become much more tolerant. But a lot of young people who live in Burnley never leave the area, so they don't know that there's a different world out there. Faith leaders sometimes walk round here, but when the kids see them, they run off. Younger imams have a chance of being heard, but the older imams have no chance. They don't talk on the right level and they don't know how to tackle the issues that are important to young people. Youth workers can engage with young kids better because they don't use faith as their starting point. Some young kids do go to mosque and they talk to each other about which mosque they go to and which sect they belong to, but when they leave junior school, they use homework as an excuse not to go, and then you see them in the streets playing football! (male Muslim aged 26 years)

Imams haven't a clue how to reach young people. All they do is lecture them. If you sat in front of an imam and said 'I've had sex with a girl', they'd judge you immediately and probably tell your parents. But younger imams are good to talk to . . . you can tell them things that you wouldn't even tell your parents. Imams are important for teaching the religion of Islam and the laws of Islam, but I'd never tell an imam that I'd taken drugs or anything . . . Youth leaders are more approachable than imams because they can give you advice about health dangers and things like that and they wouldn't be as likely to give you a religious lecture. Younger role models are good for Muslim kids 'cos they empower people and they help the person himself to make the change instead of saying 'That's wrong and you'd better change' which is what you'd normally get from an imam. (male Muslim aged 21 years)

Imams were traditionally important and still should be, but unfortunately they're not. What's happening is that a lot of imams are coming over from Pakistan and they've been born and bred there and they're completely out of touch with younger Muslims who have been born and bred here. We still have Muslim identities, but we're English and they don't really understand that. Then there's the language barrier and if this isn't addressed, it will cause real problems. It's like Abu Hamza . . . he has hardly any knowledge of Islam, but he talks the language and he's influential. People are taken in by him because he's eloquent and charismatic and he's an English speaker;

so young Muslims who aren't very knowledgeable are influenced by him. Kids who go to mosque don't understand what's being taught because the Koran is in Arabic and that's when they can become vulnerable. (male Muslim aged 26 years)

There is a considerable degree of consensus among these interviewees on the issue of whether imams are engaging effectively with young people and the challenges involved in teaching Islamic principles to Muslims in the West. Though the respondents still claimed to respect Muslim clerics, all had grave doubts about whether imams who preached in English mosques were managing to reach young people who had little identification with South Asia. This view was endorsed not only by those who had been to university or spent some of their lives outside Burnley, but by those who continued to live and work in the borough. The greater degree of respect for religious leaders expressed by the Muslim pupils who took part in the school survey could, therefore, be attributed to the fact that they were still in full-time education and had less freedom and life experience than their older co-religionists. It seems that on leaving school, a large number of Muslims begin to express their religious identities more freely and are less likely to be influenced by agents of religious socialization. While religious conviction appeared to have stood the test of time among the young Muslims I interviewed, deference to religious leaders almost certainly had not.

Time will tell whether Muslims who have grown up in the West will reject *en masse* traditional religious authority and what effect this will have on future religious leadership. In addition to their misgivings about children being taught the Koran in Arabic, almost all the interviewees felt that imams were out of touch with modern society and that young Muslims living in Britain had, like their non-Muslim counterparts, been influenced by secular forces. Within these commentaries was an implicit recognition of the difficulties in maintaining a traditional religious identity in a religiously hostile part of the world – a tension that could only be resolved by the young people themselves throughout the course of their life journeys. The data also confirmed that even those young Muslims who had spent most of their lives in close-knit communities were resistant to mosque attendance and sceptical of the longer-term sustainability of traditional Islamic leadership.

The general view was that imams needed to respond to the challenges facing Islam in the West and to the diversity of modern religious expression.

There is little doubt that the attitudes of younger Muslims towards religious leaders are different to those of older generations and the current indication is that these will continue to change. Of relevance here, however, is the difference between the role of an imam and that of a Christian minister. Within the last few decades, there have been significant changes in the ministerial duties of Christian clergy with particular regard to their pastoral responsibilities and involvement in secular public life. The reasons for these changes are clear. The decline in church attendance, the rejection of formal liturgy among younger generations, the attacks on religious authority by secular agents and the emergence of a new concept of self-empowerment have all contributed to the marginalization of Christian leaders and to the disengagement of mainstream churches from the public domain. But there are also signs that when Christian priests and ministers become involved in the life of the wider community through activities such as visiting schools and partaking in civic events, they are able to engage far more effectively with young people. Imams, on the other hand, continue to be regarded as clerical rather than pastoral/community agents and as such, their involvement in activities outside mosques takes on a rather different meaning.

The interviewees' comments about the biographical profiles of imams and the nature of clerical practice contribute much to a sociological analysis of Muslim leadership in contemporary Britain. The evidence suggests that attitudes towards religious authority are changing among a very large number of young Muslim people as opportunities for social and geographical mobility continue to present themselves. In East Lancashire, it has long been recognized among younger Muslims that many local imams have migrated from some of the poorest parts of South Asia where the structure of village life is conducive to authoritarian religious expression. Islamic organizations in the UK, however (many of which are now managed by well educated professionals), are acutely aware of the language barriers that exist in some British mosques and of the growing resistance among young Muslims towards traditional leadership. But all this is starting to change as young, articulate, English speaking imams are playing a more active role in mosques throughout the country. The extent to which these younger clerics will be able to influence the power exercised by mosque committees, the style of Islamic ministry and, perhaps most important of all, the process of internal dialogue will almost certainly have an effect on Britain's Muslim population in the future.

THE IMAMS RESPOND

Towards the end of my fieldwork, I invited two local imams; one from Burnley who had recently moved away from leadership and the other from Blackburn who continued to preach on a part-time basis, to take part in separately conducted interviews to discuss some of the issues raised by young Muslims. These two men were young, well-educated, English speaking adults who had spent most of their lives in East Lancashire. The purpose of the interviews was to establish the extent to which younger Muslim leaders were beginning to reflect on the more critical views that were being voiced within their own communities and to identify any changes in leadership strategies that they thought might be necessary. In addition to their clerical training, these two men had been involved in interfaith initiatives in their own towns – an experience that distinguished them from some of their older co-religionists who had migrated from South Asia. The fact that they identified themselves as British Muslims (attributable to their British education and socialization) suggested that they had had contact not only with a large number of Muslims born and reared in the UK, but with non-Muslims from the indigenous population. Their comments echoed some of the issues outlined above:

> I migrated to the UK with my mother when I was one and a half years old. My father was already settled here. My grandfather came here for financial reasons. In those days, there were lots of mills and factories in Brierfield and plenty of employment opportunities. I was an imam in a big mosque in Burnley for five years. At that time, I was involved in a lot of community and interfaith work and I was also on the Burnley Task Force committee which had been set up to investigate the causes of the disturbances. I was also involved in *Building Bridges*. After that, I initiated a lot of mosque visits for all the local Christians

and that was a good way of promoting interfaith dialogue . . . Working for the Lancashire Council of Mosques enables me to keep my Muslim identity. I could have applied for other jobs, but that would have meant wearing a suit and tie and this would have been difficult for me because I already had a reputation of being an imam and people still approached me as an imam . . . Faith leadership is important, but everything depends on the image of the imam. Imams need to work hard to strike a chord with the community if the second generation is to look up to him. This can't happen if the imam is unable to speak English or understand the values of young people. There are lots of imams who are already settled in the UK, but the current drive is to make sure that imams in mosques speak English and that this becomes the norm. New mosques are trying to do this. In mosques where there are Urdu-speaking imams, attempts are being made to employ imams who speak English to work along-side him . . . The Koran is very important if we are to keep the message that has been passed down for fourteen hundred years. The Arabic text is vital because it contains the original meaning and some of this cannot be translated into other languages. Anything else would only be a *translation* of the Koran. This is why we need to help people to learn the Arabic text and then give them the nearest English understanding of it. At the moment, the priority is to get people to learn the Arabic alpha-bet so that they can learn the Koran. They can learn the *meaning* of the Koran at a later stage. But very few mosques impart the meaning of the Koran. This is only really done in mudrassas . . . Most Muslims know how to follow Islamic teachings in their daily lives without necessarily knowing the Koran. Even scholars haven't been able to understand the Koran with total-ity because you could go on and on and on . . . Over the centu-ries, Islam has adapted all over the world and it is starting to adapt now in the UK because of the Muslims that now live here. Islam started off in Arabia, then moved on to Iraq, then to Persia, then to the sub-continent. It has always managed to maintain its prophetic traditions, but in some parts of the world, cultural influences have also crept in. If you take the Indian sub-continent, for example, Islam is strong there, but there are Hindu rituals at Muslim weddings! Now in the UK, modern Muslim thinkers are trying to adapt Islam to a European way of life. We know that we are now having to teach children differently. We cannot teach them in the way we would in our ancestral homelands. In South Africa, for example, the Islamic syllabus is now in English and Muslims there have adapted very well to their surroundings. I don't think this adaptability is weakening Islam; in fact, I think it's strengthening it and I think that in the future, this will give young Muslims a better sense of belonging to a whole community. My hope is that we manage to do the same here in the UK. At the moment, we are moving forward rapidly. The interesting thing is that Indian Muslims living in Britain have been able to do this much more easily than Pakistani Muslims because Indians feel less attached to their homelands because of Hindu influences. This is why Indian Muslims don't tend to send money back home. Most of what they earn goes into the British economy, but Pakistani Muslims still send some of what they earn to their relatives in Pakistan; but I'm sure that in time, this will also change. (Burnley imam aged 27 years)

In Burnley and Nelson, the majority of Muslims are from Pakistani backgrounds whereas in Blackburn, the majority are from Indian backgrounds and there are differences in how these two communities bring up their children. This can have a bearing on whether or not they attend mosque. A lot of it has to do with their education, their financial status and what's going on around them including local, national and global events, and all these things can have an affect their spiritual lives. But generally speaking, there has been in a decline in mosque attendance among young people . . . I think we need to explore new avenues in order to grasp the attention of young people and to understand who *they* are, what *their* identity is . . . There are a lot of challenges for faith leaders. Language is certainly a barrier and many young Muslims born in the UK find it difficult to understand what the imam is saying when he is preaching in the mosque. The imam needs to be bilingual and even multi-lingual. In East Lancashire, the best imams are the ones who can speak English *and* Urdu, Punjabi and Gujarati, but that's asking a lot! These days, young people are afraid to ask imams questions because they think that imams are high in status and therefore unapproachable. I think we need young enthusiasts within Muslim communities who might not have very active roles within the mosques, but who have strong community links and who could work with mosque committees in bringing communities together. I also think there is a need for English speaking imams who can act as a second in charge in mosques and who can work alongside non-English speaking imams to translate sermons from Arabic, Urdu or Punjabi into English. In Blackburn, for example, the mosques are now moving much more towards the system that they have in the South African mudrassas where the literature is also in English, so that young people are better able to understand what they are learning. I think that Muslims all over the world still need to learn Arabic because that is the language of the Koran, but it's also essential that they have access to translations. (Blackburn imam aged 28 years)

Both these commentaries convey the imams' awareness of the challenges facing Islam in modern Britain. As fully trained religious leaders, these two young men were keen to engage with local Muslims and to encourage future generations to remain faithful to Islamic teachings, yet both were aware of the limited appeal of certain aspects of Islam within their own communities. Though neither of the men were in favour of women being allowed to train for religious ministry (confirmed towards the end of the interviews) or of lay people taking responsibility for duties that Islam assigns *only* to imams (the leading of mosque prayers and the delivery of sermons, for example), both expressed support for faith partnerships and interfaith dialogue.

As far as their perceptions of clerical office were concerned, the imams recognized the value of working with other religious leaders and the need to form alliances with secular bodies. Both men were themselves regular attendees of community cohesion events and their work involved frequent dialogue with representatives of secular organizations. This suggests a greater willingness as well as a greater ability of younger, English speaking imams to engage with the wider society than one might expect to find among older clerics who have migrated from South Asian homelands. There would be much to be gained from the pursuit of sociological research that could test the generalizability of these findings and establish the extent to which they signal a new direction in Islamic leadership in the West.

THE VOICES OF YOUNG CHRISTIANS

The withdrawal of young people from Christianity can be attributed, at least in part, to the decline in deference towards religious authority. While Evangelical and Pentecostal congregations continue to attract the largest number of Christian converts in the UK, religious activity among young people in mainstream denominations (Roman Catholic, Anglican, Methodist, Baptist and Presbyterian) has reached an all time low. This begs the question of what the more conventional forms of Christianity can learn from Evangelical, charismatic and Pentecostal movements if young people are to play a more active role in faith communities – an issue that would make useful comparative research. The current indications are that revivalist movements show little interest in interfaith dialogue and that their members are often critical of established churches. With the exception of the Spirit of the North project, there was a serious under-representation of teenagers and young adults in interfaith activities in Burnley and a conspicuous absence of Evangelical Christians.

If greater involvement in religious activities is to be encouraged among younger people in the UK and, more importantly, if Christian–Muslim relations are to progress, it is imperative that the voices of young Christians are heard. While religious divisions are less pronounced than ethnic and class divisions in the UK, faith partnerships can, as the Spirit of Burnley project demonstrated, help to unite towns and cities that have been damaged by civil unrest. Despite the difficulties experienced by non-English speaking imams in engaging with second and subsequent generation Muslims, the endurance of strong religious beliefs within Muslim communities suggests that there is some potential for interfaith dialogue, as long as there are sufficient numbers of Christians to make the exercise worthwhile. While the growing religious apathy among some young Muslims is beginning to be addressed by Islamic organizations such as the Muslim Council of Britain and the Lancashire Council of Mosques; Christian organizations, because of their greater fragmentation and failure to avert the forces of secularization over a much longer period, lag behind. The attitudes of young Christians towards religious leaders could, therefore, help those denominations that have lost the most members to identify what they might do differently in the future. The following comments from three young Christian men offer some clues:

> Attitudes towards religious leaders depend on the leader himself and on your own faith. It is possible to be autonomous and not to be influenced by what other individuals say. I think there are still a lot of faith leaders out there who continue to have an influence on young people, but I'd describe myself as a freethinker. (male Baptist Christian aged 24 years)

> I've been very lucky because the minister in our church has been good at explaining things to me and he seems able to put the Bible into a context that makes sense. He had the vision to create the Basement project here in Burnley – that's a project for young people where they meet on a Friday evening, play pool, listen to music and just talk. He's trying to do the same now in other parts of Burnley. (male Methodist Christian aged 23 years)

> I think faith leaders need to meet young people in places where they can be found, like on street corners. Street pastors do this sort of thing in places like Birmingham and Manchester and it's a really good initiative. There should be evenings of entertainment for young people with music and even if you're not a Christian, it could still be good. Street pastors in Manchester really make an effort to reach young people where they're at. I'd like to start going out into the community and doing it myself, but at the moment, a lot of young people might know more than me! I think faith leaders also need to go into schools much more to try and sell the Christian message, but without forcing it. In 1997, we had an *Oasis* youth worker. The *Oasis Trust* is a Christian fellowship and their remit is to work with community groups of faith and those of no faith; but it's really a faith-based project. Within six months, the Oasis worker went into the local community and he brought in about fifty young people off the streets and the crime rates in Burnley fell. I was

only about twelve at the time, but looking back now, I realize what a big effect he had on my faith. The leading officer of the Boys Brigade also had a big effect on me because he used to do really interesting Bible talks and bring it to life. (male Baptist Christian aged 21 years)

Like their Muslim counterparts, these respondents expressed little support for ascetic religious tradition and all were critical of the dogma associated with high churches. To some extent, it could be argued that their views reflect the turbulence that has occurred within Christianity since the early-1970s manifest in the questioning of ecclesiastical authority, disagreement between religious clerics over key aspects of Christian doctrine and falling church attendance. At the same time, it should be recognized that these interviewees were themselves citizens of a modern liberal society that allowed them freedom of expression and the choice of how (or even whether) to put their religious beliefs into practice. In contrast with those who adopt a more conservative religious stance, these young Baptist and Methodist Christians seemed to be making an implicit appeal to faith leaders to engage with young people at grass-roots level and to take the gospel message into schools, community centres and, most ambitious of all, onto the streets.

All the Christians I interviewed agreed that young people growing up in modern secular society were less willing than ever before to acquiesce to religious rules.[5] One point that was frequently made was that even Christians who were baptized in infancy, attended faith schools and associated with members of the same denominations were, with the exception of a very small minority, moderate in their religious convictions. If these assertions are correct, the implications for Christian leadership are very far-reaching. Priests and ministers who are keen to encourage younger people to play a more active role in Christian communities may need to examine the current religious landscape through new lenses and create opportunities that have never previously existed. Needless to say, this will depend as much on the structure and organization of the faith community as on the leader's readiness to give younger people a greater stake in the life of a parish or congregation. A more pessimistic view is that young people have no real interest in church activities and there is very little that even the most progressive clergymen or women can do to reverse this situation. Perhaps, then, the time has come for Christian leaders to adopt a more innovative approach to their ministry.

At this juncture, it is worth mentioning that even those who belonged to the conformist churches expressed a greater preference for experiential events such as pilgrimages, retreats and residential conferences than for high worship. Roman Catholic and Anglican interviewees, for example, were mildly critical of some of the beliefs and practices of their own churches, and although they continued to attend weekly mass or communion services, their main motivation for doing so was to keep their relatives (particularly their parents) happy. Like the other respondents, these young church goers were keen to share their religious perspectives not only with Christians of other denominations, but with members of non-Christian faiths and even with secular thinkers who were willing to give them a voice. This suggests that faith sharing opportunities for young people in the future may present themselves in more secular forms (a process that seems to have already begun) as the voluntary sector continues to expand and new partnerships are formed. The most likely scenario will be that while some young people will continue to embrace Christian beliefs and attend the churches into which they were baptized, others will seek alternative forms of spiritual nourishment.[6]

Community projects that welcome the participation of faith groups will almost certainly present new opportunities for Christians and Muslims to form alliances, but as yet, it is difficult to say what form this dialogue will take. Nor is there any way of knowing how religious leaders will respond. Given the secular nature of these initiatives, it is unlikely that faith communities will bring anything other than a humanitarian perspective to bear on the formation of what is essentially a strategy for reducing conflict. If my prediction is correct, the approach that faith groups will adopt will be not unlike the one I described in Chapter 3 in which the value of human diversity is acclaimed not through sermons, liturgies or sacred texts, but through an inclusive code of ethics.[7] Who knows whether this will win the support of religious leaders? Though there are synergies between ethical and religious philosophies, this may be altogether too subtle an approach for imams whose primary responsibilities are to lead prayers and impart Islamic teachings. My hunch is that it will be lay Muslims

already employed in the public and voluntary sectors (NGO officers, youth leaders and others) who will continue to represent the
Islamic faith in cohesion initiatives. Christian leaders, on the other
hand, may begin to play a more active role in the work of faith
partnerships not least because their ministerial duties take them to
the heart of (very diverse) local communities. But they too may
not be willing to support secular projects with the same enthusiasm. Parish priests who are concerned with maintaining the apostolic tradition, for example, may be less willing to embrace change
than street pastors and community chaplains who tend to work
more closely with different social groups and whose religious
and secular roles are often fused. With such a complex and fast
changing landscape, the future of religious leadership and the
involvement of Christian leaders in faith partnerships could be
very interesting indeed.

THE GENDER QUESTION

It would be remiss of any sociological study of religious cohesion
to ignore the views of women on issues of religious leadership.
Within Islam, the position of women is gaining new prominence
in the UK for a number of reasons. Since the 1980s, more Muslim
girls have gained entry into higher education and into the world
of employment. For these younger Muslim women, this has led
to more frequent social migration and renewed aspirations. Notwithstanding the cultural inhibitions with which some Muslim
girls continue to battle within their own communities, there can
be little doubt that the legislative changes introduced by the
British government during the latter half of the twentieth century
and the subsequent occupational mobility that has been achieved
by Muslim and non-Muslim women alike have raised expectations on a large scale. Whatever inequalities may still exist, there
are now more positive role-models of Muslim women in western
societies than at any other time in history. But the social and
cultural representations of Muslim communities and the attitudes
of Muslim women towards their own leaders (political and religious) are often anything but positive.

In the autumn of 2006, there was a surge of media interest in
faith and ethnic group relations when Jack Straw, MP for Blackburn

with Darwen, made a controversial statement about Muslim women who wore veils and the effect he believed this was having on community relations. Mr Straw suggested that the wearing of veils was detrimental to community cohesion in areas of the country that were blighted by segregation and he went on to explain how Muslim women visiting his Blackburn surgery would sometimes be asked to remove their veils before a consultation. Mr Straw's comments provoked a range of reactions among Muslims and non-Muslims alike and the debate (which was forced into the open with immediate effect) continued for several months. Contrary to popular myth, a sizable number of Muslim women who cover their faces are articulate, well-educated and socially ambitious – evidence if ever we needed it, that Muslim communities are themselves very diverse.[8] If religious cohesion is to include women as well as men, these gender issues cannot be ignored.

It is worth emphasizing that even the most professionally accomplished Muslim women often hold strong religious beliefs and maintain close family ties. In very few cases does their career success, even on relocation to a university town or city, cause them to abandon their beliefs or to date non-Muslims? Like their male counterparts, however, Muslim women demonstrate different degrees of adherence to their faith. During the course of my investigation, I met several professional Muslim women who admitted to missing daily prayers and/or to breaking the rules of fasting during Ramadan, though none had transgressed (or claimed to have done so) serious Islamic prohibitions such as taking drugs, consuming alcohol or engaging in pre-marital sexual intercourse. The women did, however, hold different views on faith schools, the wearing of veils and the Sharia penal code.

The views of Muslim women on matters of faith leadership are gaining importance, not only because women make up half the world's population, but because Muslim women are often involved in religious activities in their own towns and cities and, more significantly, within their own families.[9] The following interview data reveal striking similarities in the views of three of these women on the authority of imams and the effects of Islamic teachings on gender relations:

Islam is not quite as far behind Christianity in its secularism, but it's certainly changing. What's happening at the moment is that people are becoming either extremely religious or they're just going the opposite way and rejecting religion completely. Some Muslims are brainwashed by imams 'cos they worry themselves sick about the Day of Judgement! Others become religious because they find it a comfort. Imams are still in mosques, but they're losing their power among Muslims. I don't follow any particular imam because a lot of them have come from abroad and not all of them are British educated. It becomes a real problem when an imam tries to preach something, but Muslim children have read different things 'cos they're educated and they question much more than their parents. Young people want evidence now and they'll ask imams where something is written in the Koran and then they start to realize that it's all about interpretation. Children will listen to a certain extent, but things are changing rapidly. (female Muslim aged 27 years)

There are some imams who I wouldn't listen to because they say that the mosques should be closed to women and I think that contradicts Islamic teachings. A lot of Muslims still respect imams, but mosque committees have a lot of control over what imams are allowed to do. Young people now need to start setting their own agenda, even if this differs from elderly people, because it's only by doing this that younger Muslims will start to learn from their own experiences. The same people often take the lead and it's nearly always imams and male committee members and this doesn't always give young women the confidence to come forward. (female Muslim aged 24 years)

It's different for a woman than a man because women don't usually attend mosques. Men look up to imams because they attend mosque. When I was little, my mosque teacher was a lady and she taught me Arabic, but I didn't really learn much about Islam. I can read Arabic but I can't translate it, so I don't really understand what I'm reading. That's why I'd rather read the Koran in English. Some older people, including many imams, believe that it doesn't matter if you don't understand what you're reading because it's the Arabic that's important. A lot of Muslim parents get upset because their children now speak English and it's hard for people to learn the dominant language and to learn about their religion at the same time. I think modern imams need to be able to speak both languages and to offer the English translation of the Koran even though they claim it can't easily be translated. I remember some years ago when I first heard an imam speaking in English and I thought 'wow!'. He was really involved in education and he was also good with computers. My brothers went to him for Arabic lessons, but it was also great that he could speak English . . . I suppose my role models are my parents. They set the best example of how I'd like to practice my faith; but there are no women faith leaders in Islam and that's one of the problems. (female Muslim aged 26 years)

All three women bemoan the inability of imams to engage effectively with young people and all are critical of the leadership practices in local mosques. It is also clear from these accounts that while mosques in Burnley may not have been typical of elsewhere, a large number seemed to exclude women – a practice that validates the view that mosques are patriarchal organizations that serve as meeting places for men and/or that they encourage male-only worship. Unlike many Christian denominations, Islam does not allow women to enter the religious ministry and at the time of the investigation, there were few if any women serving on mosque committees. There is growing concern, particularly among younger Muslim women, that unless these gender inequalities are addressed, the capacity-building potential of religious cohesion strategies will be limited.

At present, the opportunities for young Christian women to partake in church activities seem far greater than the opportunities available to Muslim women to partake in the life of the mosque. This suggests that the religious initiatives in which Muslim women are more likely to be involved are community rather than mosque oriented – an increasingly common scenario in East Lancashire due to the expansion of the voluntary sector into which younger Muslim women are now starting to move. This raises the issue of whether, and in what ways, religious leaders, both Muslim and Christian, will lend support to initiatives that attract female volunteers. The following views of five young Christian women, all of whom were actively involved in voluntary projects in and around Burnley between 2005 and 2007, suggest that priests and ministers have varying degrees of influence on younger people in the Christian tradition and that faith partnerships may well take a new direction:

> I don't think about the role of faith leaders to be honest. Jesus is really the leader of my life. But I must admit, when I went to Canada and I saw Pope John Paul, words couldn't express what I felt. It was a great feeling. But faith is part of my life and I don't think too much about leaders. The priest is just an agent. (female Roman Catholic aged 25 years)

> Faith leaders have devoted their lives to their faith and I do take in a lot of their sermons. Most of the ministers have been influential in my life and I suppose that's mainly because they've been close friends and mentors. I have looked up to famous Christians such as Martin Luther King as good examples to follow . . . I'd say I have a lot of respect for people who devote their lives to their faith. (female Baptist aged 23 years)

> I went to a Christian-based youth work conference not so long ago and we did seminars where leaders talked to us and it was really good. There were Bible studies and all sorts of things. But I want to go to a church that has lots going on and ministers can sometimes influence that, but I think it's the congregation itself that makes the Christian community rather than the minister. (female Baptist aged 18 years)

> Faith leaders don't really have an impact on me, but they can affect the values that you have and I think that's important. A lot of the youth work I'm involved in has a faith element, but most of the projects are run by youth leaders rather than faith leaders. One of the programmes I'm involved in is run by Christian people, but they're more like youth workers than Christian ministers. (female Anglican aged 22 years)

> I respect faith leaders, but there are two priests at my church and one is younger than the other and I can relate to him more than the older priest. When I left school, I went on a retreat and I got talking to a priest and he talked about how he used to doubt and everything and somehow, it made him seem more human. But I don't think I'd turn to a priest if was in trouble or something. I'd probably turn to my family for help. (female Roman Catholic aged 19 years)

With the exception of the second respondent, these women felt that Christian leaders were largely ineffectual. It is worth noting that it was those who belonged to the non-conformist rather than the Roman Catholic and Anglican churches who were most likely to be influenced by religious ministers, but even here, the influence was not significant. There are several possible reasons for this, some of which echo the explanations for the declining influence of imams in some mosques. By far the most convincing explanation is that young people in the West, including those who have received some form of religious socialization in childhood, are influenced by a huge array of secular trappings and spend large parts of their lives in the secular sphere. Within the mainstream Christian tradition, young people have inherited these secular influences from their own parents and it seems that younger Muslims too are being influenced by this process at virtually every stage of their lives.

From a gender perspective, the implications of these findings should not be underestimated. If, as the interviewees' comments suggest, traditional religious leadership is losing its stronghold in Britain, and if indeed there is little gender variation in attitude towards religious leaders, there is every reason to believe that women will have as much influence as men on the religious identities of young people in the future and may even take a leading role in the work of faith partnerships. The increasing employment of women in NGOs should, if the current evidence is anything to go by, create more opportunities for women to become involved in faith initiatives. The comments of the fourth interviewee above offer the strongest clues for how these opportunities will most likely present themselves. This young Anglican woman was an active youth worker whose religious faith clearly underpinned her secular responsibilities, but it is her reference to the nature of her work rather than to her beliefs that signifies the likelihood of these changes. While this may seem like little other than an attempt to secularize religious activities, it is becoming abundantly clear that the potential for Christian and Muslim leaders to engage not just with each other but with younger people lies not so much in patriarchal ministry, but in opportunities presented by secular bodies. Women in both the public and the voluntary sectors look set to steer this course.

LEADERSHIP IN AN EDUCATIONAL FAITH CENTRE:
A HOLISTIC APPROACH

In March 2005, Lancashire County Council's plans for a major school rebuilding programme triggered some unprecedented changes in Burnley that would take faith into uncharted territory. The main funding source for the programme was the Building Schools for the Future (BSF) capital investment budget introduced by the government to support the transformation of secondary education in England and Wales.[10] In essence, the eight previous high schools were closed and five 11–16 mixed schools were established with an additional sixth form located on a separate site.[11] These new establishments opened in August 2006.

Burnley and Nelson qualified for more than £200 million of funding on the grounds of deprivation, low attainment and that fact that the school buildings were in need of modernization. There were also concerns of a political nature about school admissions policies and parental choice (Burnley Borough Council, 2006). According to the borough council's own literature, the Burnley Task Force had identified dissatisfaction among some parents about school admissions criteria – an issue that had resulted in a growing number of parents choosing to send their children to schools outside the borough. The Task Force found that the ethnic composition of schools had become a more significant factor in parental choice than ease of travel or educational attainment (ibid.). Whatever the truth of this, it was hoped that the BSF programme would, in addition to achieving its principal aims of raising aspirations and attainment and improving opportunities, help to foster good community relations and create a greater sense of unity between the town's two main ethnic groups.

The six new establishments were located on previous school sites while the building work was ongoing. The *Burnley Schools' Sixth Form* was also established on one of the original school sites along with a faith centre. This faith centre would offer a range of activities and resources to children, young people and older residents in the Burnley and Pendle boroughs. The purpose of the faith centre was to provide a facility that reflected the multicultural/multifaith diversity of the town and a focal point for anyone with (or even without) an interest in faith issues.

It was clear from the outset that if the objectives of the faith centre were to be met, some attention would need to be given to human as well as physical resources. As part of its commitment to the restructuring of the high schools and the establishment of the new sixth form, Lancashire County Council appointed a faith co-ordinator to work with schools, local authority officers and other agencies across the Burnley and Pendle boroughs in organizing and facilitating activities. These included conferences and curriculum support for primary to sixth form students, community workshops, religious services (mono-faith as well as interfaith), feasts and celebrations, seminars, faith sharing forums and a range of other activities that aimed to build positive community relations. The success of the faith centre would depend largely on the ability of the co-ordinator to forge links with key players such as head teachers, religious leaders (particularly Christian and Muslim clerics), youth workers, project managers, county council representatives and other practitioners.

There was no doubt that the establishment of the faith centre would present groups such as BBB, BBP, Churches Together and the Lancashire Forum of Faiths with an opportunity to work with Lancashire County Council and thus promote their constitutional objectives. In turn, the faith centre would benefit from the involvement of a network of partner organizations. It has already been mentioned, for example, that in April 2006 (some 5 or so months before the appointment of the faith co-ordinator), BBB appointed three part-time workers for a twelve month period – a faith leadership officer, a young people's officer and a women's officer. Moreover, the *Bridge* project (resourced and managed by BBB and renowned for its outreach work in primary schools) had been up and running for several years, offering curriculum support and after-school provision. If pooled effectively, this wide range of human resources could bring much to bear on faith relations in and outside education.

In order to support to the faith co-ordinator in meeting the county council's objectives and to make known to all relevant stakeholders its potential to contribute to the development of the faith centre, BBB established a New Schools Working Group. Since BBB representatives were aware that the co-ordinator's role was to facilitate faith provision rather than to lead religious worship (hence the title *co-ordinator* rather than *chaplain*), one of their priorities was to offer a chaplaincy service that would include pastoral support. The absence of available funding, however, meant that provision of this kind would, like most of the other faith centre activities, be dependent on the willingness of faith leaders to visit the centre on a voluntarily basis. Since the schools and colleges in Burnley and Pendle recruited students from both religious and secular backgrounds, the kind of activities that would be provided at the faith centre would be determined not only (perhaps not even) by religious membership but by the interests of the students themselves.

The faith centre comprised a small foyer, an office, an ablution area for Muslim worshippers, a quiet place for prayer, reflection and meetings and a large function room for conferences, celebrations, and spiritual activities. The centre as a whole was tastefully decorated and newly carpeted and, considering its temporary nature, provided a suitable space for the delivery and facilitation of curriculum, faith and other community events. Its neutral interior bore all the hallmarks of a multi-purpose meeting place that could be used for religious and secular activities alike.

Within a short time of his appointment, the co-ordinator met with his colleagues and other interested parties to outline the county council's objectives for the faith centre as part of the BSF programme and to consider how some of the provision might be extended to the wider community. While it would have been too ambitious at this stage for the co-ordinator to consider how 'faith' in all its guises might be included, he was eager to offer a facility that would allow young people to share their spiritual, moral social and cultural perspectives.

By the end of the first term, the co-ordinator had hosted a number of events and activities at the faith centre which aimed to unite people from all social backgrounds. In this initial period, the success of the faith centre depended largely on the co-ordinator's ability to make use of the resources available and to organize events and activities that would attract the largest possible audiences. These included an opening service, a Ramadan awareness workshop, a joint Christmas/Eid party, an advent celebration and a *Question Time* evening. These events demonstrate how people from different communities can, with appropriate support, learn about each other's cultural and religious traditions. For many young people in British schools and colleges, these opportunities are few and far between.

Though it is difficult to quantify the success of what is essentially qualitative provision, there can be no doubt that in the first few months of its opening, this new faith centre managed to attract the interest of schools, community leaders, sixth-form students and members of the general public. The events and activities that took place in this initial period were aided by the efforts of the BBB young people's officer, a local youth leader and a large number of volunteers who helped with planning and publicity. The extension of the faith centre to the wider community also created a serendipitous opportunity for the young people involved in the Spirit of Burnley project to tour their exhibition. At the same time, and in order to support not only the future development of the faith centre but some of the other work in which they were involved, five BBB members embarked on a residential programme of study entitled *Issues in Ecumenical and Multifaith Chaplaincy* at Ushaw College, Durham – a course for in-service chaplains, youth workers and religious volunteers with an interest in the development of interfaith initiatives. Time will tell whether this faith centre will be a success, but in the last analysis, the effectiveness of faith cohesion strategies in educational settings such as these will depend not on religious revival, but on the ability of faith leaders (and/or faith co-ordinators) to adopt a holistic perspective. It seemed that Lancashire County Council's faith centre in Burnley was able to offer a social space that could accommodate cultural, ethnic and religious diversity and that allowed those who occupied it to define spirituality in their own way.

ENGAGING WITH THE WIDER COMMUNITY

In addition to the progress made at the *Burnley Schools' Sixth Form*, religious leadership took a variety of other forms in East Lancashire at the time of the investigation. Some of the initiatives were dialogical in nature, involving the discussion of faith in public settings, while others were more experiential, examples of which included school twinning projects, interfaith festivals and educational workshops. By the end of the investigation, partnerships between faith communities and other voluntary organizations had evolved to such an extent that it was becoming impossible not only to keep abreast of all the initiatives that were being launched, but to distinguish between religious and non-religious activities.

In 2006, the BBB women's officer and the young people's officer spearheaded a small number of initiatives that reflected new ways of thinking about how faith communities could contribute to secular society and to the objectives identified by the recently established Commission on Integration and Cohesion.[12] The most successful initiatives for women resulted from the formation of a women's focus group, a youth and community girls' group and a women's skills group. These groups had two broad objectives; first, to provide a forum for women from different cultural and religious backgrounds to share common interests in spaces where there would be no men present (an approach that was, by its very nature, attentive to the experiences of older Muslim women) and secondly, to engage with women who were difficult to reach including economic migrants, the elderly and non-English speaking women who had little contact with communities other than their own. Between the summer of 2006 and the spring of 2007, the BBB women's officer organized a number of events including a mosque visit and a calligraphy workshop for non-Muslim school children, a multifaith celebration day, a lecture entitled *An Evening with Inspirational Women*, a humanitarian fundraising appeal and several public seminars on the representation of women in different religious traditions. These events met with varying degrees of success. The mosque visits for school pupils were well received not least because they were presented as aesthetic rather than pedagogical activities. The voluntary events, on the other hand, tended to appeal to targeted groups or to those with a specific interest in the issues concerned – a situation that sometimes resulted in an imbalance in ethnic and faith group representation and/or a low turnout of participants. These shortcomings aside, there was no single event that failed to create an opportunity for dialogue.

The role of the young people's officer coincided so much with that of the women's officer that during the first few months of their employment, the two officers worked together in the planning and delivery of interfaith activities. At the half way stage of her employment, the young people's officer was seconded by BBB to spend one full day a week at the sixth form in order to offer some assistance to the faith co-ordinator and to help tour the Spirit of Burnley exhibition. For the remainder of her time, she attended a series of community cohesion workshops and contributed to the planning of four further initiatives – a *Faith in Action* exhibition, a Shrove Tuesday celebration, a customs and culture workshop[13] and an event to commemorate the Prophet Muhammed's birthday. These events and activities were publicized at the Burnley Carnival, the Cultural Festival, the East Lancashire Together Convention and the Community Cohesion Conference hosted by Burnley Action Partnership. It is forums such as these that provide third and voluntary sector groups with some of the best opportunities to discuss their work and to and establish new partnerships.

The most successful capacity building initiatives, however, are those that promote cohesion between as well as within boroughs. In 2005, the Anglican Diocese of Blackburn received some funding from the Faith Communities Capacity Building Fund to sponsor two programmes, both of which aimed to create a better understanding of religious diversity in Lancashire. The first of these was entitled *The Faith to Faith Exchange* – an 8-week programme of interfaith dialogue hosted by the Outreach and Development Agency of Blackburn Cathedral. Each session lasted for 1 hour and comprised a verbal exchange between representatives of different faith communities. All eight sessions were held on weekday afternoons and admission was free to the general public. The first four sessions involved an Anglican priest in dialogue with a Muslim development officer from the Lancashire Council of Mosques,[14] while the next four sessions extended the dialogue to representatives of the Jewish, Hindu, Sikh and Buddhist communities. Each session comprised 40 minutes of conversation between the two speakers followed by 20 minutes of audience participation. Discussions revolved around sacred texts, religious observances, rituals, pilgrimages and religious unity. The size of the audience ranged from 50 to around 130 attendees. The sessions took place in Blackburn Cathedral and were filmed by a group of Media Studies students from Blackburn College of Further Education.

The second programme comprised six bi-monthly seminars entitled *Looking Back at Anger*, all of which were held in different venues in Burnley, Blackburn, Preston, Lancaster and Blackpool.

Each seminar (approximately three hours in length) was led by two or three guest speakers and facilitated by a representative of the Board for Social Responsibility.[15] The seminars included guest talks, audience participation and plenary sessions for reflection and comments. The speakers addressed issues of community cohesion and relayed strategies deemed by various stakeholders to have had a positive effect on public relations throughout the region. Like the Faith to Faith series, the most popular of these seminars attracted around one hundred and thirty attendees.

While both of these programmes were funded for only a short period of time, they were successful in uniting people of different ages and from different ethnic and religious communities. As one might expect, the events attracted a disproportionate number of senior citizens (attributable to the fact that the sessions were held during the day), although the 30 or so college students who attended the Faith to Faith series invited their friends and relatives. The overall success of the programmes lay not so much in the number of people they attracted, however, but in the ability of the speakers to address religious issues from social, cultural and political perspectives. In the Faith to Faith series, conversations revolved not only around religious beliefs, but family and kinship ties, educational initiatives, the economy, neighbourhood renewal policies and community relations. The Looking Back at Anger seminars addressed the issues of religious and political extremism, media propaganda, free speech, social democracy and citizenship. The central themes of integration, diversity and social justice underpinning both these programmes created more potential for networking than would have been the case had they been tailored to reflect the interests only of religious groups. Initiatives such as these present faith communities (lay people as well as religious leaders) with a long-awaited opportunity to engage with the wider society.

Summary

This chapter has highlighted the changing attitudes of young people towards religious leaders and the issues to which these changes give rise. It is clear that leadership takes different forms within as well as between faith communities and that each community has its own way of promoting its beliefs. My research suggests that while religious convictions were stronger among Muslims than Christians in East Lancashire, attitudes towards religious leaders were changing in both communities. I have also argued that there is a gender dimension to these attitudes which should not be overlooked. Muslim men were far more likely than Muslim women to have contact with imams (though not necessarily with lay leaders), and this may help to explain the misgivings that some Muslim women had about traditional religious authority as they grew older. The Muslim women I interviewed, however, were insistent that the patriarchal practices about which they spoke were cultural rather than religious in origin and that gender inequalities were contrary to the teachings of Islam. In contrast, Christians of both sexes experienced less intense religious socialization than Muslims and this needs to be borne in mind when attempting a comparative analysis of religious attitudes.

What, then, are the likely effects of these young people's views on faith leaders and what form is religious leadership likely to take in the future? The answers to these questions lie in how religious clerics view their roles and in their attitudes towards secular modernity. Imams conduct most of their ministry in close-knit communities where beliefs and worship are taken seriously and where koranic texts are used to impart Islamic teachings. Whatever resistance younger Muslims may be starting to demonstrate against these traditions, their belief in God and in the basic tenets of Islam remain steadfast. Christian clergy, on the other hand, are aware of the more difficult challenges within their (comparatively) diverse communities, not least of which is how to encourage younger people to become more involved in faith-based activities. Despite these challenges, there were a number of initiatives in East Lancashire that presented religious leaders with an opportunity to work together and to establish closer links with secular agencies. These initiatives included dialogical exchanges in places of worship, the facilitation of interfaith projects for young adults, outreach work in education and the formulation of strategies that helped local authorities to address civil unrest. If these strategies and initiatives are to achieve sustainability in the longer term, however, religious leaders will need to galvanize the support of lay people and other community activists.

Notes

1 There were 25 of these in 2006.
2 www.interfaith.org.uk
3 Particularly the government's proposal to close places of worship which were believed to be involved in the propagation of religious extremism.
4 A youth group involved in community activities and overseen by the Lancashire County Council Youth Service.
5 This was borne out, though to a slightly lesser extent, in the interviews with young Muslims, most of whom regarded daily prayer, studying the Koran, fasting during Ramadan and attending mosque as tedious and demanding exercises.
6 For a more detailed analysis of this process, see Heelas and Woodhead (2004).
7 Woodhead and Heelas (2000) distinguish between three types of religious organization: *Religions of Difference*, *Religions of Humanity* and *Spiritualities of Life*. This typology is an attempt to classify religious organizations in accordance with cultural expressions and offers a useful framework for what I am describing here. Many faith groups that form partnerships belong to religions of difference, yet in order to make an effective contribution to secular initiatives, they need to adopt expressions more akin to religions of humanity.
8 In 2006, a number of fully veiled Muslim women in Burnley and Blackburn took part in some local seminars (most of which were for women only) about the wearing of the veil in public places.
9 In Britain, for example, it is Muslim women who tend to be responsible for teaching children the Koran at home.
10 The funding was secured by Lancashire County Council who took responsibility for leading the programme.
11 This new sixth form was a separate institution from Burnley College of Further Education located approximately one mile away.
12 This 'think tank' was established by the Labour Government in August 2006. The aim of the Commission was to consider how local areas could respond to diversity and some of the tensions that it could cause.
13 A curriculum enrichment activity for a group of students enrolled on a Level 2 Travel and Tourism programme at Burnley College of Further Education.
14 In April 2007, this (female) development officer was the first Muslim to be appointed to the cathedral's community cohesion team.
15 A sub-group of the Outreach and Development Agency.

6. Reflections and conclusions

Throughout this book, I have identified a number of religious cohesion strategies and described how some of these were implemented in Burnley and Blackburn at the time of the investigation. Educational underachievement, the erosion of manufacturing industries, derelict housing and family breakdown did little to ease the social divisions that existed in East Lancashire at the time of the investigation or to prevent the enclavization of BME communities.[1] The segregation of ethnic groups, minority and majority, was responsible for an inward looking parochialism and the alleged formation of 'parallel lives'. There were, and still are, casualties on both sides of this unfortunate divide. As long as racist attitudes among an unyielding core of the indigenous White population on the one hand and the insularity of a smaller but significant number of Asian residents on the other remain unaddressed, these divisions look set to continue. It is little wonder that the appeal for integration expressed in the language of community cohesion is high on the government's agenda.

Bleak though ethnic relations in the north of England seem, there is some reason for optimism. It is not impossible for members of BME groups to live in enclaves yet still feel that they are British citizens. My research shows that despite their strong religious convictions and spatial enclavization, most of the Asian Muslim pupils who took part in the school survey expressed loyalty to the UK and to the values with which Western liberal democracies have come to be associated. There are, of course, liberal values that challenge certain Islamic traditions, and those values must prevail.[2] On this issue, the British government and other public bodies need to be clear that their commitment is to protect the democratic rights of the individual in the face of pressures from Muslim factions in pursuit of a theocratic state. In the main, however, the

Muslims who took part in the investigation supported the values of liberal democracy and felt that Britain was their home.

For members of the White indigenous population who express strong nationalistic sentiments, the challenges are rather different. Views of racial superiority (evidenced in the survey results of School A) are more commonly held among members of lower socio-economic groups for whom social exclusion is a source of resentment. Unlike many BME residents who are enclaved as a result of past-war settlement or personal preference, the White working classes (including those not working) are often forced into enclaves because of their dependence on social housing or the privately rented sector. In spaces such as these, White people have little or no contact with members of BME communities which means that their prejudices (propagated by far right groups such as the BNP) are seldom put to the test. My research suggests, however, that religious cohesion strategies, where they are delivered through public services, can be effective in helping members of the White majority population to overcome their fear of difference and adjust to demographic changes. For all its shortfalls, Citizenship Education is able to aid this endeavour as are NGOs and statutory bodies which claim some success in improving community relations.

How, then, can *faith* communities help to create a cohesive society? I have identified three different models of religious cohesion in this book – the contributory, the experiential and the dialogical – none of which is mutually exclusive. Each of these models represents a different way of promoting religious unity in multicultural, multi-faith areas of the UK. The contributory model emphasizes the potential for people of faith to work with secular agencies in the formulation of policies that strengthen community cohesion and avert civil conflict. I have argued, however, that representatives of faith groups need to refrain from using religious language if they are to increase their chances of being included in these consultations and of quelling misconceptions about the reasons for their interest. The opportunities for faith partnerships to contribute to secular initiatives are numerous. Among the examples I have offered are school outreach work, secular projects that include faith perspectives and local authority strategic planning. The principles advanced by this model aim to foster closer working relationships between religious and secular agencies in a liberal democratic society.

Unlike the contributory model, the experiential model is applicable mainly to people of faith, though there are some initiatives that welcome the participation of non-believers.[3] In essence, the experiential model emphasizes the importance of learning about different religious beliefs through activities that produce empathy. While the experiential model appeals to a narrower group of people (mainly religious devotees) than the contributory model, its capacity building potential is greater than it seems. In Chapter 4, I described how a group of young adults who took part in an interfaith project known as *The Spirit of the North* shared a weekend of residential activities as a way of demonstrating their support for religious unity. At the end of the project, the participants created a public exhibition that attracted a large audience and led to the formation of new partnerships. At a time when tensions are running high and where segregation is damaging the image of a large number of British towns, the need for religious cohesion has never been greater. Statutory and voluntary organizations would do well to support experiential initiatives whenever the opportunities arise.

The dialogical model is the most formal of the three and emphasizes the importance of serious debate. At the level of leadership, open dialogue offers the best and in some cases, the *only* opportunity for faith leaders to discuss their respective doctrines. For the theologically erudite, formal dialogue is essentially a scholarly activity that enhances knowledge and aids the discovery of truth. But interfaith dialogue is not just for trained religious leaders or for those skilled in theological acumen. In Chapter 5, I offered some examples (there are many more) of dialogical exchanges in which lay people can also be encouraged to participate. The 'Faith to Faith' series held at Blackburn Cathedral, the 'Looking Back at Anger' regional seminars organized by the Anglican Board for Social Responsibility and the Question Time event hosted by the staff and volunteers of the *Burnley Schools' Sixth Form* attracted faith leaders and laity alike. Of the three models, the dialogical places the most emphasis on opportunities that allow people of faith to air their doctrinal differences.

Although these models show that different religious cohesion strategies can work for different groups of people, they address largely the same objectives – the pursuit of a society in which religious diversity is valued. My hope is that the models will provide a better understanding of how faith communities can help make these objectives a reality. The social benefits that faith initiatives can bring in uniting people in segregated towns constitute more than a general nod in the direction of integration. Unlike the United States, Britain does not have a form of civic religion that centres on one nation and this makes religious unity all the more difficult to achieve.[4] Though interfaith initiatives reach only a small minority of the population, faith partnerships can help to ameliorate social divisions and beat down the prejudices that make these divisions seem inexorable.

However committed the government might be to the concept of community cohesion, there is no established policy for dealing with religious conflict; nor would it be easy to frame one. In any case, segregation in the north of England is a consequence not so much of religious, but of cultural and ethnic divisions exacerbated by economic inequalities and compounded by deeply internalized prejudices. When tensions occur, it is often (though by no means always) the result of people's misguided perceptions of social justice and the feeling that those who are in a position to make a real difference are impervious to life on the edge. While political activists continue to fight these inequalities through conventional secular processes, the challenge for faith partnerships is to devise strategies that will help to diffuse these tensions and extol the strengths of a multifaith, multicultural Britain. The following principles provide a useful framework for how this work might begin.

Faith partnerships in a secular society: the way forward

LOCAL KNOWLEDGE

Knowledge of the area in which a faith partnership is about to be established is an essential criterion for success. Initially, this may be little more than a cursory mapping of the religious landscape and some general inquiries into whether faith-based initiatives have previously been attempted. One of the main strengths of the Spirit of Burnley project, for example, was that the organizers channelled their efforts into creating a product that would capture the interest of local stakeholders. As it happened, the sixteen participants were members of only two faith communities, and while this may not have presented the best opportunity to learn about faith systems other than Christianity and Islam, it did unite young people from some of the town's most enclaved wards. Moreover, those involved in the project were aware of local changes that would provide an avenue for publicity, the most significant of which was the restructuring of the high schools and the establishment of an educational faith centre. By creating exhibition products that could be used for curriculum enrichment, the participants aimed to mobilize the support of local students and raise the profile of faith through Citizenship Education.

Over and above their ability to adapt to their own town or city, faith partnerships need to establish links with secular agencies if they are to make their work known to the wider community. Between 2001 and 2007, BBB publicized its achievements through the Burnley Arts Festival, cultural awareness days (hosted by a number of local high schools), the East Lancashire Together Convention, the Burnley, Pendle and Rossendale Council for Voluntary Service, the New Schools Working Group, the Burnley Action Partnership, the Burnley Community Network and the Lancashire Council of Mosques. Local knowledge, it seems, is the key to maximizing the potential of faith groups to contribute to community cohesion and attract new recruits.

TRANSFERABILITY OF SKILLS

The skills of individual members are essential for the effectiveness of faith partnerships. Like most other NGOs, BBB and the BDIC attracted people who were experienced in planning and facilitating community activities. There is no doubt that the employment of around half the members in the voluntary sector and the other half in either full-time education or public services strengthened the ability of these partnerships to achieve their mission. The skills that the members amassed in their educational and employment roles manifested themselves in most if not all the initiatives in which the partnerships were involved. These included the ability to identify aims and objectives, work in teams, set targets and facilitate group tasks. The leadership positions held by some of the members strengthened the pool of expertise and provided the kind of experience needed for the management of interfaith programmes. There can be no question that the transferability of skills from the statutory to the voluntary sector enhances the success of faith partnerships and should, therefore, be advanced as a guiding principle.

USE OF THE MEDIA

Despite its secular orientation, the media can make an important contribution to religious cohesion both locally and nationally. On the whole, local newspaper companies and radio stations presented the activities of BBB and the pivotal work in which it was involved in a positive manner. *The Burnley Express* and the local free newspaper *Burnley Now* publicized interfaith feasts, faith awareness events and the Spirit of Burnley project, all of which showed greater rather than lesser degrees of success.[5] In Blackburn, *BBC Radio Lancashire* invited representatives of the BDIC and the Outreach and Development Agency of Blackburn Cathedral to comment on some of the initiatives in which they too had been involved. These examples demonstrate the ability of the media to inform the general public of events and initiatives that promote cohesion.

While no one would deny that radio stations and newspapers are powerful sources of communication, it is important for faith partnerships to tread carefully when dealing with people who work in the media industry. Ever mindful of the nature of their audiences, journalists and editors are often sceptical of the objectives of faith groups and tend to regard religious beliefs as incongruous with modern secular society. Be this as it may, most of the mass media continue to include religious issues in their programmes and allow people of faith a voice. For their part, faith communities need to ascertain the cultural and political orientation of broadcasting companies before requesting air time or agreeing to take part in media interviews.

THE ROLE OF RELIGIOUS LEADERS

Religious leaders have much to contribute to community cohesion, but the nature of their involvement in the present climate warrants serious reflection. Although Christian and Muslim clerics played an instrumental role in the formation of BBB after the 2001 disturbances, religious leaders are often regarded as ineffectual among large numbers of young adults. The ground, it seems, is shifting towards the emergence of new structures and innovative styles of religious leadership. The most successful initiatives are those facilitated by lay people rather than religious clerics. The examples I have provided in this book include school outreach work (facilitated most successfully in East Lancashire by Building Bridges Pendle), after-school programmes, the Spirit of the North project and community events such as those organized by the staff and volunteers of the Burnley Schools' faith centre. It is worth reiterating that the success of initiatives such as these lies not so much in their ability to tackle religious differences, but to explore faith perspectives through humanitarian issues.

My research suggests that if religious clerics are to make a serious contribution to the work of faith partnerships, they will need to re-connect with young people and support some of these strategies. In segregated northern towns where expectations are generally low and where the events of 2001 are all but forgotten, it is imperative that Christian and Muslim leaders work as closely as possible with lay people in creating opportunities that reflect the interests of the wider community. Where religious convictions range from very strong to non-existent, this is a difficult but not an impossible mission.

LINKS WITH THE WIDER COHESION AGENDA

By far the greatest challenge for faith partnerships is how to engage with wider secular society. Though this raises important issues about the relationship between the public and the private sectors, the community cohesion agenda is providing new opportunities for faith partnerships to contribute to public relations. This is not to suggest that faith groups have never attempted to do this or that they are instrumental in engendering public disaffection, but the irony of civil conflict in enclaved towns is that faith communities can, with sufficient will, contribute in ways that they may never previously have considered.

The language of community cohesion and the issues with which it has come to be associated – regeneration, neighbourhood renewal, bridge-building, conflict resolution and so forth – have sown the seeds for interfaith activities, though the process of *intra*-faith dialogue is far from complete. While faith communities may have had difficulty in engaging with each other in the past, the real and sometimes visible consequences of religious and ethnic conflict have highlighted the need for greater awareness and understanding. But if faith partnerships are to have an impact in the longer term, they will need to attract more people. Interfaith initiatives that focus *only* on doctrinal issues are unlikely to appeal to anything other than a small number of (religious) recruits. For those initiatives that aim to explore similarities and differences between faith communities, reference to religious doctrines is unavoidable. But for initiatives that are guided by a more holistic mission, there are several ways in which faith perspectives can be incorporated into a programme without losing the support of those for whom it is primarily intended.

As far as faith partnerships are concerned, the first and probably most essential strategy is to adopt a language that will appeal to those who do not hold conventional religious beliefs. This will depend as much on the religious and secular profile of the location as on the way in which the initiatives are marketed, but the chances of attracting large numbers of (particularly young) people to initiatives of an explicitly religious nature are becoming increasingly slim. To the die-hard traditionalist, of course, surrendering religious concepts is tantamount to denying the existence of a omnipotent deity, but those willing to embrace social change (including secularization) will see this as an opportunity to explore common values without attempting to undermine the beliefs of individuals. By appealing to people of all faiths and none, faith partnerships can celebrate unity and diversity at one and the same time.

Commendable though this might be, faith partnerships are still faced with the problem of how to attract religious exclusivists. The answer, it seems, is that they cannot. Devotees of fringe groups who are on a mission to impose a theocratic world view on the rest of humanity tend to regard faith cohesion initiatives as an opportunity (if not a duty) to win new recruits to their own cause. For most religious fundamentalists, interfaith groups are well-meaning but ineffectual organizations that seek social pleasantries at the expense of real truth. While this may be the view of a small minority, it signifies the need for members of faith partnerships not only to identify common ground, but to hold robust conversations about their religious differences. Needless to say, those who hold exclusive views may find this an altogether too threatening experience.

For those who are willing to meet the challenge of promoting religious cohesion through secular avenues, there is much scope for progress. There are several nationwide community cohesion initiatives that have paved the way both for public services (particularly health, education and the police service) and voluntary groups to address social divisions. The time has come for all those involved in community cohesion to stand united. In East Lancashire, some of the most successful events have been launched by NGOs working in consultation with statutory bodies. These events include arts festivals, cultural awareness days, road shows, carnivals, celebrations, charity galas, extravaganzas, annual conventions and many others. While most of these are cultural rather than religious in orientation, they provide faith partnerships with an opportunity to engage with secular organizations. The ability of faith communities to adapt to a modern pluralistic society where individual choice is celebrated and all manner of life options are available will be the acid test of their effectiveness.

In the end, the most important requisite for social harmony is something that transcends rational discourse. Whatever the efforts of voluntary groups, statutory bodies and local councils to achieve community cohesion and however determined faith partnerships might be to stamp out intolerance, it will be ordinary people living in ordinary neighbourhoods who will have the final say. Social conflict invariably erupts at grass-roots level (though it is often exacerbated by local, national and international politics) and it is here that it will need to be resolved. As I bring this book to a close, I am mindful of the deepening segregation of the communities about which I have been writing and of the parallel lives to which this is starting to lead. The smouldering resentment among parochial indigenous groups on the one hand and the crisis of identity among some young British Muslims on the other remains a potentially potent mixture. If disturbances were to break out again in the north of England, it could hardly come as a surprise. In Burnley, BNP activists continue to propagate a distorted nationalistic ideology, while elsewhere, Islamic extremists impart a message of violent *jihad* to a small but growing number of vulnerable recruits. Though no one would deny the importance of dynamic leadership, it will, I believe, be the hearts and minds of people living in these segregated towns that will make the decisive difference.

Notes

1 For a more detailed analysis of the enclavization of Asian and White communities in these East Lancashire towns, see Billings and Holden, 2007 and 2008.
2 Traditional Islamic views on homosexuality and (in some cases) the role of women, for example, would result in discrimination if ever they were to be reflected in British law.
3 In Chapter 2, I referred to non-believers who were willing to take part in faith initiatives as *secular integrationists*.
4 In its attempt to redefine national identity, the British government has now introduced citizenship tests and ceremonial rites of passage for economic migrants from other lands seeking permanent residence.
5 The Spirit of Burnley project received attention both from *Radio Lancashire* and *The Burnley Express*. The *Radio Lancashire* broadcast comprised a ten minute interview with three of the participants while the *Burnley Express* published a short newspaper article on the Whalley Abbey conference and the exhibition launch.

Appendix 1 Building Bridges Burnley: origin and evolution of a modern faith partnership

Building Bridges Burnley (BBB) was formed in 2001 in partial response to the disturbances. The committee of the Burnley Lane Fellowship of Churches (a local group of Trinitarian Christian denominations) wrote to offer support to Muslim leaders who were trying to restore calm in areas of the town where the violence had occurred. Several weeks later, leaders from the Roman Catholic Church, the Church of England, the Methodist Church, the Free Churches and the local Islamic community formed a united group and the first Christian–Muslim partnership was born. Between the early autumn of 2001 and the spring of 2003, the organization evolved from a handful of individuals to a formally registered charity.

Throughout the development of the partnership, BBB sought representation on a number of statutory and voluntary committees including the Council for Voluntary Service, the North West Forum of Faiths, Social Services, the Inter Faith Network for the UK, Burnley Community Alliance, the UK Islamic Mission, the Islamic Foundation, East Lancashire Together and a large number of other bodies involved in interfaith and/or community cohesion initiatives. Some of these organizations offered financial as well as administrative assistance to the partnership and helped to create opportunities for the promotion of positive public relations. In the early stages, however, the primary objective of BBB was to assuage the tensions fuelled by the disturbances.

In May 2004, BBB appointed its first full-time co-ordinator and a part-time clerical officer and an office was established on the ground floor of a local mosque. This mosque later became the official BBB centre. An adjacent room was made available some months later for committee meetings and for the execution of clerical duties. This was the first (and the time of this investigation, the *only*) mosque in the North West of England to facilitate a Christian–Muslim partnership and to allow non-Muslims access to its premises. In the initial stages of his appointment, the BBB co-ordinator spent most of his time attending strategic planning meetings, preparing funding bids and developing a programme of activities. By 2005, the organization had received funding from the Single Regeneration Budget, the Children's Fund, the Tudor Trust, Islamic Relief, the Methodist Church and several hundreds of pounds in donations from some smaller charities. While most BBB committee members were employed in the voluntary sector, those engaged in pastoral and community work (particularly religious ministers and youth officers) were becoming increasingly involved in the organization's initiatives.

At the time of the investigation, the BBB partnership comprised four committees (that is, a management committee and three sub-committees). The management committee consisted of around 25 people (including some auxiliary members) who met on a bi-monthly basis. The purpose of this committee was to monitor the organization's accounts and to preside over the three subcommittees. The first sub-committee was responsible for the facilitation of the *Bridge* project – an initiative for children between the ages of 8 and 13 years which became formally incorporated into BBB in April 2005. The second sub-committee, known simply as *The BBB sub-committee*, played a key role in the planning and implementation of interfaith events and activities for adults in and around the town. The third sub-committee – *The New Schools Working Group* – was involved in the provision of faith activities in the town's five newly formed high schools and in an evolving Sixth Form. The Bridge project, because of its mission to provide after school activities for children living in some of the most deprived wards of Burnley, attracted the lion's share of the organization's funding. Between its formation in 2001 and the official starting date of this investigation in 2005, BBB had launched a series of Christian–Muslim seminars, several church and mosque visits, an interfaith feast and a tsunami appeal.

Alongside these activities and events, the Bridge project contributed to community cohesion by providing a programme of activities for school children at risk from social exclusion. The project officers (five in all) worked closely with schools and other agencies and had, in the previous 4 years, provided activities for several hundred children. The main aim of the project was to engage children in community orientated activities such as sport, drama, teambuilding and outdoor pursuits. Between 2002 and 2005, the Bridge team had delivered eleven after-school programmes, more than 20 free holiday activities and several residential workshops to children living in deprived areas. By the end of 2005, there were ten primary schools and a small but growing number of secondary schools involved in Bridge activities.

The progress made by BBB was evidenced in the committee's own minutes and evaluation documents. What had begun as a largely reactive partnership in the months following the disturbances had become a proactive one within a 4-year period. The organization had gained recognition for its work at local, regional and national levels and had received visits from interfaith groups in Sheffield, Leicester and Northern Ireland. It was clear from the amount of funding that BBB had received and from the positive relations that it had established with local agencies that it had made a positive contribution to community cohesion.

Appendix 2 The religious and ethnic composition of Burnley

In the first year of the investigation, a large amount of demographic research was undertaken in order to establish some basic details of the borough; details such as the size of the local population, the religious and ethnic composition of the wards, the profiles of the residents, patterns of migration and changes in the local economy. These details revealed strong clues about the evolution of the borough and the deprivation that the local council was trying to address.

The data confirmed that for several decades, Burnley had had to contend with a large number of social and economic problems. According to the 2003 Mid Year Population Estimates, the overall population of the town had been in decline since the early-1990s. Between 1991 and 2001, the number of inhabitants fell from 91,148 to 89,541 due to an unusually high level of migration among young people between the ages of 15 and 29 years (Burnley Borough Council, 2005a). By 2006, the figure stood at 88,100 (Burnley Borough Council, 2006). Current estimates suggest that if this trend continues, there will be only 82,700 people living in the borough in 2028 – a decline that is atypical of the wider region. At the time of my research, the figures showed a higher than average number of children living in Burnley, but a relatively small number of adults between the ages of 20 and 40 years. The figures for ethnic membership were also significant. The BME population had increased from 5 per cent in 1991 to 8.2 per cent in 2001 with a growing number of Asian residents (including married couples) in the younger age groups (ibid.).

In addition to these demographic changes, the data revealed strong evidence of segregation. The 2004 Deprivation Index (cited in Burnley Borough Council, 2005b) confirmed that Burnley fell within the top fifty most deprived local authorities in the country and that this deprivation manifested itself in housing, health and education. While in the few years prior to the investigation a small number of Asian residents had begun to purchase properties in wards that had previously been occupied by members of the indigenous White population, spatial segregation between ethnic communities remained pronounced. In 2001, the main ethnic groups living in the borough were, in descending order, White British (90.11 per cent), Pakistani (4.94 per cent), Bangladeshi (1.58 per cent) and Indian (0.48 per cent). The Caribbean, Chinese and African communities constituted only 0.25 per cent collectively (Census, 2001). The concentration of the town's Pakistani and Bangladeshi residents confirmed the extent of the ethnic divisions that clearly still existed.[1]

Predictably, the 2001 Census revealed a close relationship between religious and ethnic membership. The town's 6.6 per cent Muslim population was drawn from the Pakistani and Bangladeshi communities, while the 74.5 per cent of 'Christian' residents were predominantly White British. Despite this close religious-ethnic group relationship, however, there was no knowing the levels of faith conviction within the two communities. In view of the decline in Christian church attendance and the suggestion that a growing number of second and subsequent generation Muslims in Britain are reluctant to attend mosque, there seemed little point in using institutional worship as the main indicator of religiosity.[2] This problematic relationship between religious beliefs and religious practice is one of the reasons directors and facilitators of interfaith initiatives prefer to use the term *spirituality* – an inclusive concept which encompasses all forms of religiosity.

Although the opportunities for interfaith dialogue vary from locality to locality, the bipolar composition of Burnley and the absence of any interfaith activities prior to 2001 made it a prime location for the investigation. The suggestion that the people of Burnley were living in mono-cultural enclaves, fuelled, in some cases, by the politics of envy, supported the view that this was a town characterized by fear and mistrust. Almost every voluntary sector convention in the town between 2001 and 2005 made stark reference to the lack of political engagement between local agencies, alarming levels of social exclusion, low social aspirations among young people and, perhaps most disturbing of all from the point of view of community cohesion, the success of the British National Party in winning seven seats on the local council. The formation of BBB was the first real attempt by the Christians and Muslims of Burnley to address these difficult issues.

Notes

1 Seven of the eight mosques were situated in one of these wards – a ward in which there were no churches. In the remaining 14 wards, there were 38 churches and only 1 mosque.
2 There are, in any case, no official mosque attendance statistics available in the UK; hence, any attempt to establish the extent of institutional participation among young Muslims would have involved onerous quantitative research. I decided, therefore, to explore *attitudes* towards religiosity (rather than frequency of church and mosque attendance) through semi-structured interviews.

Appendix 3 The comparative town: Blackburn

In the early stages of the investigation, it was decided that one of the best ways of evaluating the success of interfaith activities in Burnley was through comparative research. The town that was chosen for comparison was Blackburn – another mill town some 10 or so miles west. By comparing two industrial northern towns, both of which had a sizable Muslim population, more empirical evidence could be collected and more weight added to the analysis.

The similar industrial landscapes of Burnley and Blackburn were not the only reasons they were chosen for comparison. From a religious cohesion perspective, Blackburn had, in the years preceding the investigation, launched a number of initiatives that had been successful in mobilizing faith communities into action. The Blackburn with Darwen Interfaith Council (BDIC) was established in 2004, and in 2005, several school partnership schemes were introduced in the town in the hope of improving faith and ethnic relations among primary school children. The BDIC had also invested a considerable amount of time trying to engage with people of no faith and encouraging faith leaders to play a more active role in civic events; hence, it was clear that the BDIC had adopted similar interfaith strategies to BBB. What was not known was how these strategies had been implemented or if they had been successful. By comparing the initiatives of both towns, a better understanding of religious cohesion would hopefully be achieved.

The 2001 Census revealed that 77.9 per cent of the residents of Blackburn were White British, 10.7 per cent were Indian and 8.7 per cent were Pakistani. Christians constituted the largest faith group of the town (63.3 per cent) followed by the Muslim community of 19.4 per cent (ibid.). Despite the differences in ethnic group composition between Burnley and Blackburn and the fact that Blackburn was a much larger borough with a population of 137,470 residents, there were similar levels of educational underachievement and strong evidence of spatial segregation.

In both towns, the biggest majority of the Asian residents lived in the most deprived wards. The Daneshouse and Stoneyholme ward of Burnley and the Bastwell and Shear Brow wards of Blackburn were known by indigenous White locals as Asian (or 'Paki') ghettos. All three wards had shops, restaurants and places of worship that had been established by the Indian, Pakistani and Bangladeshi communities during the 1960s and 1970s. As one might expect, most of the schools in these wards were attended by Asian children – a pattern of educational recruitment that had gradually changed the ethnic profiles of state and voluntary-aided schools alike. This was a consequence not only of Asian settlement, but of the actions of White parents who had made a conscious decision to send their children to schools on the outskirts of town (or even in other boroughs) where there were fewer Asian pupils. This White flight response to the presence of British Asians in primary and secondary schools had done little to aid public relations.

Appendix 4 Ward descriptions: Daneshouse and Stoneyholme and Rosehill with Burnley Wood

The Daneshouse and Stoneyholme ward

Daneshouse and Stoneyholme was a central ward that was situated in the north of the town centre. The ward was within one half mile of the main shops and was surrounded by several busy roads that linked the town to the motorway networks. In 2005, there were over 6,000 people living in Daneshouse and Stoneyholme, making it one of the most densely populated wards in the borough. The most striking feature of the ward was the exceptionally high number of young residents (due mainly to a high birth rate) and the very low number of people over the age of 60. Of all the wards in Burnley, Daneshouse and Stoneyholme was home to the largest number of people under the age of 30 and the smallest number of residents over the age of 45 (Census, 2001).

Daneshouse and Stoneyholme was by far the most deprived ward in the town. Like many other wards in East Lancashire, it was once inhabited by a thriving population of textile workers. Almost all the houses in this ward were Victorian terraces divided at the rear by cobbled or concrete gangways. A small number of the properties had garden areas, but most were pavement fronted. Between 2001 and 2003, there were around 550 empty dwellings in the ward and the house prices remained among the lowest in Lancashire. At the time of writing, there were several empty properties deemed unfit for dwelling and awaiting demolition. The ward also had one of the highest rates of arson and domestic burglary.

The ethnic group composition of Daneshouse and Stoneyholme had changed considerably since the mid-1960s. Around two-thirds of the properties were occupied by Pakistani or Bangadeshi residents, making it the most mixed ward in the borough (ibid.). Most of the Pakistani residents lived in Daneshouse along with a small number of indigenous locals, many of whom were elderly and had lived in the area most of their lives. The Bangladeshi residents lived mainly in Stoneyholme. Though there had, from time to time, been tensions between some of the younger residents of the ward, people tended to live amicably.

There were a variety of local shops and businesses in the Daneshouse and Stoneyholme ward owned by Asian proprietors and patronized by Asian communities. These included grocery stores, halal butchers, gents' and ladies' hairdressers, jewellers, hardware shops, clothes shops, newsagents and travel agents. The ward was served by two mixed schools for children aged between 4 and 11 years and a newly established Sixth Form. Since 2001, youth workers, sports leaders and community development officers had expended a large amount of effort in mobilizing young people into civic participation. An increasing number of these workers were of Asian heritage with considerable influence in their own communities and who were regarded as role models. Since the 2001 disturbances, Burnley Borough Council and the Council for Voluntary Service have encouraged the active recruitment of young Asian males into positions of leadership. The high degree of heterogeneity *within* as well as between ethnic communities, however, presented an additional challenge to project leaders who needed to be ever mindful of the fact that segregation had an internal as well as an external dimension.

Rosehill with Burnley Wood

Rosehill with Burnley Wood was a central ward situated South East of the shopping centre. Although the ward was similar in size to Daneshouse and Stoneyholme, its ethnic and religious profiles were very different. Rosehill with Burnley Wood was home to a slightly larger number of residents (around 6,600 in total), the majority of whom were White British. The ward was populated by a wider range of age groups than Daneshouse and Stoneyholme (Census, 2001).

Rosehill with Burnley Wood had a complex deprivation profile. Around one third of the ward (that is, the Burnley Wood rather than the Rosehill area) fell into the lowest 20 per cent of deprived wards in the borough, with approximately one third of this falling into the lowest 5 per cent (Burnley Borough Council, 2003). As such, it was one of the principal areas identified in Burnley Borough Council's 15-year plan for urban regeneration. Like many other inner wards in the borough, a large number of houses in Burnley Wood were privately rented.[1] Prior to a major housing regeneration programme in 2003, the area was characterized by high turnover rates compounded by the constant movement of families and couples abandoning neglected properties.[2] The area also had high rates of drugs offences and arson offences. In contrast with Burnley Wood, Rosehill was a much more affluent part of the ward with more valuable properties, lower rates of crime and stronger health profiles. In socio-demographic terms, this confirms that Rosehill and Burnley Wood was a heterogeneous ward in which socio-economic background had a significant effect on life chances.

The deprivation profile of Burnley Wood and the problems to which this had given rise led to the formulation of a number of community initiatives in the area between 2001 and 2007. Among the most successful of these were the *Street Level Project* and the *Neighbourhood Learning Scheme*, both of which aimed to involve disaffected young people in skills-based activities. The bulk of the funding for these initiatives was provided by local enterprise groups, the Northwest Development Agency, the European Regional Development Fund and various local authority departments. Most community projects in the ward were co-ordinated by a team of development workers at the local *One Stop Shop* – a Limited Company that offered a range of activities including a women's group, an art group and a lunch club. Among the facilities were a cyber café, a Credit Union and free internet access.

There were three main places of worship in the Burnley Wood part of the ward, all of Christian orientation. These included two Anglican churches and a Roman Catholic church. The two Anglican churches were approximately 400 m apart and their parishes extended to the neighbouring wards of Brunshaw, Bank Hall and

Trinity. In line with the national trend, there had been a sharp decline in weekly church attendance and other religious activities at these churches since the early 1970s to the extent that their main support lay in the hands of a few remaining parishioners. Sunday services in all three churches attracted less than 100 worshippers, most of whom are elderly people and a small number of young families.

If the secularization thesis is to be measured in terms of falling religious participation, there is no doubt that it would be supported in Burnley Wood. The high degree of religious indifference along with the absence of Asian Muslim residents accentuated its White, working-class image. Like Daneshouse and Stoneyholme, this ward bore all the hallmarks of a deprived community in which there was little religious activity.

Notes

1 Most of these were stone-built terraced properties.
2 In 2003, more than 350 houses in this ward had been abandoned as a result of strained relations between landlords and tenants.

Bibliography

Aldridge, D. and Halpern, S. (2002), *Social Capital: A Discussion Paper*, London: Performance and Innovation Unit, Cabinet Office

Alibhai-Brown, Y. (2000), *Beyond Multiculturalism*, London: Foreign Policy Centre

Battle, J. and Grace, G. (2006), *Citizenship Education: A Catholic Perspective*, London: University of London

Baubock, R. (2002), 'Liberal Pluralism Under Attack', in *Cohesion, Community and Citizenship*, London: Runnymede Trust, pp. 54–71

Baumann, G. (1996), *Contesting Culture: Discourses of Identity in Multi-ethnic London*, Cambridge: Cambridge University Press

Billig, M. (1995), *Banal Nationalism*, London: Sage

Billings, A. and Holden, A. (2007), 'The Contribution of Faith to Integration and Cohesion and the Threat Posed by Enclavisation in Some Northern Towns' – think piece published by the Department of Communities and Local Government: www.communities.gov.uk, June

Billings, A. and Holden, A. (2008), 'Interfaith Interventions and Cohesive Communities: The Effectiveness of Interfaith Activity in Towns Marked by Enclavisation and Parallel Lives'. Final report submitted to the Home Office and the Department of Communities and Local Government

Blunkett, D. (2003), *Civil Renewal: A New Agenda*, London: Home Office

Building Bridges Pendle (2002), *Building Bridges Pendle Interfaith Schools Programme*, (unpublished)

Burdsey, D. (2006), "If I Ever Play Football, Dad, Can I Play for England or India?' British Asians, Sport and Diasporic National Identities', *Sociology*, 40(1), 11–28

Burnley Borough Council (2001), *Burnley Speaks, Who Listens . . . ? A Summary of the Burnley Task Force Report on the Disturbances in June 2001*, Burnley: Burnley Borough Council

Burnley Borough Council (2003), *A Neighbourhood Renewal Strategy for Burnley*, Burnley: Burnley Action Partnership

Burnley Borough Council (2005a), *Social and Community Cohesion: Strategy and Action Plan 2005–2007*, Burnley: Burnley Borough Council

Bibliography

Burnley Borough Council (2005b), *Burnley Snapshot 2005: Facts and Figures at a Glance*, Burnley: Burnley Borough Council

Burnley Borough Council (2006), *Burnley 2006: The Real Story*, Burnley: Burnley Borough Council

Cantle, T. (2001), *Community Cohesion: A Report of the Independent Review Team*, London: Home Office

Cantle, T. (2004), *The End of Parallel Lives?: Final Report of the Community Cohesion Panel*, London: Home Office

Cantle, T. (2005), *Community Cohesion: A New Framework for Race and Diversity*, Basingstoke: Palgrave Macmillan

Catholic Education Service (2007), *Survey on Chaplaincy Provision for 14–19 Year Olds in Catholic Schools and Colleges in England and Wales*, Available online http: www.cesew.org.uk

Census (2001), Office for National Statistics

Centre for Local Economic Strategies (CLES) (2005), *Spirit of Blackburn Evaluation Document*, Manchester: CLES

Coles, M. I. (2004), *Education and Islam: A New Strategic Approach*, Leicester: SDSA

Credo Consultancy (2003), *Key Facts from the 2001 Census*, Preston: Credo Consultancy

Frankenburg, R. (1966), *Communities in Britain*, Harmondsworth: Penguin

Giddens, A. (2002), *Runaway World: How Globalisation is Reshaping Our Lives*, London: Profile Books

Gilchrist, A. (2004), *Community Cohesion and Community Development*, London: Runnymede Trust

Goodhart, D. (2004), 'Too Diverse?' *Prospect*, February, pp. 30–37

Heelas, P. and Woodhead, L. (2004), *The Spiritual Revolution: Why Religion is Giving Way to Spirituality*, Oxford: Blackwell

Hewitt, R. (2005), *White Backlash and the Politics of Multiculturalism*, Cambridge: Cambridge University Press

Holden, A. (2002a), *Jehovah's Witnesses: Portrait of a Contemporary Religious Movement*, London: Routledge

Holden, A. (2002b), 'Witnessing the Future: Millenarianism and Postmodernity', *Sociology Review* 11(3), 28–31

Holden, A. (2007), 'The Burnley Project: Faith Attitudes among Young People in Burnley and Blackburn', *Faith Initiative* issue 17 May 2007

Home Office Faith Communities Unit (2003), *Partnership for the Common Good: Interfaith Structures and Local Government*, London: Inter Faith Network for the UK

Home Office Faith Communities Unit (2004), *Working Together: Co-operation between Government and Faith Communities*, London: Inter Faith Network for the UK

Bibliography

Inter Faith Network for the UK (2006), *The Inter Faith Network for the UK 2005–226 Annual Review*, London: Inter Faith Network for the UK

Kateregga, B. D. and Shenk, D. W. (1980), *Islam and Christianity: A Muslim and Christian in Dialogue*, Nairobi: Uzima Press

Kazi, M. and Eades, J. (2005), *Integrating Empirical Practice Procedures: Realist Evaluation of the Building Bridges Interfaith Project in Lancashire, England,* (unpublished)

Lancashire County Council (2004), *Our Vision for Education in Burnley: Burnley Schools for the Future,* Preston: Lancashire County Council

Leonard, M. (2004), 'Bonding and Bridging Social Capital: Reflections from Belfast', *Sociology,* 38(5), 927–44

Local Government Association (2002), Office of the Deputy Prime Minister, Home Office, Commission for Racial Equality and the Inter Faith Network (2002), *Guidance on Community Cohesion,* London: LGA Publications

Local Government Information Unit (2005), *Scrutiny of Community Cohesion Issues,* London: LGIU

Mitchell, C. (2006), 'The Religious Content of Ethnic Identities', *Sociology,* 40(6), 1135–52

Modood, T., Berthoud, R., Lakey, J., Nazroo, J., Smith, P., Virdee, S. and Beishon, S. (1997), *Ethnic Minorities in Britain: Diversity and Disadvantage,* London: Policy Studies Institute

Morrissey, M. (2003), 'Briefing Paper: A Diagnostic Tool for the Analysis of Community Tension' unpublished

Northwest Development Agency (2003), *Faith in England's Northwest: The Contribution made by Faith Communities to Civil Society in the Region,* Manchester: DTZ Pieda Consulting

Northwest Development Agency (2005), *Faith in England's Northwest: Economic Impact Assessment,* Manchester: DTZ Pieda Consulting

Office of the Deputy Prime Minister (2004), *Making it Happen: The Northern Way,* London: ODPM

Office for Standards in Education (OFSTED) (October 2005), *Annual Report of Her Majesty's Chief Inspector of Schools for 2004/5,* Available online http://live.ofsted.gov.uk/publications/annualreport0405/4.2.3.html

O'Keeffe, B. and Zipfel, R. (2007), *Formation for Citizenship in Catholic Schools,* Chelmsford: Matthew James

Patel, H. (2007), 'Don't Judge Us All by the Actions of a Few', *Lancashire Evening Telegraph,* Friday, 22 June 2007

Putnam, R. D. (2000), *Bowling Alone: The Collapse and Revival of American Community,* New York: Simon and Schuster

Bibliography

Qualifications and Curriculum Authority (QCA) (1997), *About Citizenship,* Available online www.qca.org.uk/7907.html

Tonnies, F. (1887), *Gemeinschaft und Gesellschaft,* (translated as Community and Society), London: Routledge (1955)

United Religions Initiative (2001), *The United Religions Initiative Charter,* San Francisco: CA

Watch Tower Bible and Tract Society of Pennsylvania (1983), *United in Worship of the Only True God,* New York: Watch Tower Bible and Tract Society of New York, Inc.

Watch Tower Bible and Tract Society of Pennsylvania (1993), *What is the Purpose of Life: How Can You Find It?,* New York: Watch Tower Bible and Tract Society of New York, Inc.

Wilmore, N. (2005), 'Engaging With Young People', *Local Government Chronicle,* 14 April 2005

Woodhead, L. and Heelas, P. (2000), (eds), *Religion in Modern Times: An Interpretive Anthology,* Oxford: Blackwell

Woolcock, M. (2001), 'The Place of Social Capital in Understanding Social and Economic Outcomes', *Isuma: Canadian Journal of Policy Research* 2(1), 11–17

Index

Index

Index

socio-economic group 48, 49, 173
  see also social class
Spirit of Blackburn 94–8, 130–1
Spirit of Burnley 98–128, 129,
  130–1, 153, 168, 175–6, 181
Spirit of the North 23, 93–4, 95, 153,
  174, 178
Spiritual Journey Groups 19
spirituality 19, 61, 65, 92, 93, 95,
  129, 130, 133, 166, 186
statutory agencies 18, 24
stereotyping 57, 86
Straw, Jack 157–8
Street Level Project 192
suffering 104, 141
suicide bombing 40 *see also* Holy
  Wars; international terrorism;
  terrorism
Sunni Muslims 114
survey data 5, 27, 47–58, 85–6,
  135, 145 *see also*
  questionnaires
symbolism 29, 68, 104, 120, 142

team building 39
terrorism 15, 28, 53, 95, 135,
  140 *see also* Holy Wars;
  international terrorism;
  suicide bombing
textile industry 1
Thatcher Government 60
theocracy 172
Three Faiths Forum 25
Tonnies, F. 24
Trinity ward 193

Tudor Trust 183
tutorial system 71–4, 79

UK Islamic Mission 182
umma 107
United Reformed Church 16
United Religions Initiative 91–4, 95,
  96, 97, 98, 99, 100, 101, 124,
  128, 131
urban regeneration 4, 55, 179, 192
  see also social regeneration

validity 27
veiling 67, 68, 158, 171 *see also*
  hijab
voluntary groups/organizations 7, 13,
  24, 126, 132, 136, 142, 167, 168,
  174, 180 *see also* volunteers
volunteers 17–18, 138, 160, 178
  see also voluntary groups/
  organizations

weltanschauung 40
Whalley Abbey 99–100, 101, 123,
  124, 130, 181
White flight 38, 48, 189
Wicca 96
Woodhead, L. 171
world renunciation 40
worship 17, 26, 33, 35, 50, 61, 62,
  65, 87, 101, 103–4, 109, 129,
  131–2, 142, 160, 164, 170, 193

Zipfel, R. 89
Zoroastrianism 16